The Big Ü

Realising the Potential of Your Life

Laurence Udell & Tom Evans

2QT Limited (Publishing)

First Edition published 8th August 2018 by

2QT Limited (Publishing)
Settle, North Yorkshire BD24 9RH United Kingdom

© The Big Ü
Realising the Potential of Your Life

www.thebigu.me

© Copyright 2018 Laurence Udell & Tom Evans
The right of Laurence Udell & Tom Evans to be identified as the authors of this work has been asserted by them in accordance with the Copyright, Designs and Patents Act 1988

There are two ways copyright applies to this book. You can choose which you ascribe to.

The New Way
If you by chance come across a copy of this book without paying for it, buy a print, ebook or audio then gift it to someone else. All reviews also help to keep things spinning. Good ones make an author's day. Not so good ones help authors improve their writing. This all helps to keep everything in karmic balance.

The Traditional View
All rights reserved. No part of this publication may be reproduced, stored in or introduced into a retrieval system, or transmitted, in any form, or by any means (electronic, mechanical, photocopying, recording, or otherwise) without the prior written permission of the publisher. This book is sold subject to the condition that it shall not, by way of trade or otherwise, be lent, resold, hired out, or otherwise circulated without the publisher's prior consent in any form of binding or cover other than that in which it is published and without a similar condition including this condition being imposed on the subsequent purchaser.

Front cover image © shutterstock.com

Printed by IngramSpark.

A CIP catalogue record for this book is available
from the British Library
ISBN 978-1-912014-44-6

In honour, and with unconditional
love and blessings to
Amanda Elizabeth Eleanor Udell

Acknowledgements

From Laurence

Amanda Elizabeth Eleanor Udell for our paths coming together to walk all of the straight road to the truth to the very end and giving me the greatest gift possible, Unconditional Love.

Garreth and Marcus for their incredible meaningful love, care, sharing and all the crazy and amazing adventures we have together.

Sue Evans for our very special friendship, all the feedback, professional eye and quality contribution. Knowing when to ground me and when to let me fly.

From Tom

To Louise for the infinity of time and space you give me to make books like this happen.

To Insight Timer for their role in getting the whole world meditating, one person at a time, and helping Tom transition from author to internationally known meditation guide.

From Both Of Us

Big thanks to Amanda Riley for forging the connection between Laurence and Tom.

Thanks to baton carriers of the past who helped us write this book and baton carriers of future, some of whom we hope will have read this book.

And finally to our clients, we respect, honour and thank you from our hearts and souls for your openness to self discovery; your strength of mind in taking responsibility for your lives; your determination to be honest and authentic; for believing in yourselves that you can change and the courage to move forward with conviction. You have given us the pride and passion for who we are and what we do.

Contents

Acknowledgements	v-vii
Foreword	1
About this book	5
Success by other means	7
How this book is structured	9
Reasons why	11
Mechanics of how	11
Energies to embrace	12
Caveats	12
Caveat 1	13
Caveat 2	13
Caveat 3	13
Caveat 4	14
Time to awaken	14
Companion Meditations	17
Journaling	18

Part One - The Material World

The Material World	23
The Goldilocks Zone	24
Stop the world, I want to get off	26
Behind the mask	28
Why 1: It's easier	30
Why 2: The time is now	33
Why 3: It opens new doors	36
Why 4: It scales	39
How 1: Take responsibility	42
How 2: Be honest and authentic	44

How 3: Belief and trust	46
How 4: Take action	48
Energy 1: Observing and witnessing	50
Energy 2: Courage and curiosity	52
Energy 3: Sensitivity	54
Energy 4: Daring greatly	56
Key Takeaways	58
Companion Meditation: Being Grounded	58
Questions To Ponder	58

Part Two - Duality

Duality	63
In two minds	64
The tip of the iceberg	65
Soul and ego	67
Why 1: Hardship is an illusion	70
Why 2: Changing times	73
Why 3: Making a difference	76
Why 4: You have a dream	79
How 1: Time and space	82
How 2: Success and fulfilment	84
How 3: Seek and discover	86
How 4: Focus and stillness	88
Energy 1: The power of the breath	90
Energy 2: Synchronisation	92
Energy 3: Power centres	94
Energy 4: Entering the flow state	96
Key Takeaways	98
Companion Meditation: Whole Mind Harmonisation	98
Questions To Ponder	98

Part Three - Superconsciousness

Superconsciousness	103
Moving Consciousness	104
Entanglement and de-tanglement	106
A new freedom	108
Why 1: Fire in your belly	110
Why 2: Supreme performance	113
Why 3: Explosive creativity	116
Why 4: Harmony and grace	119
How 1: Let your soul lead	122
How 2: Get in alignment	124
How 3: Source-ery	126
How 4: Pure and simple	128
Energy 1: Unconditionality	130
Energy 2: Prescience	132
Energy 3: Opening to channel	134
Energy 4: Precognition	136
Key Takeaways	138
Companion Meditation: Accessing Superconsciousness	138
Questions To Ponder	138

Part Four - Oneness

Oneness	143
Unravelling The golden thread	144
Tuning into Oneness	147
Why 1: The honour	149
Why 2: The absolute why	152
Why 3: Wholeness	155
Why 4: The gift	158

How 1: Purity of consciousness	161
How 2: The end of the ego	163
How 3: Be here now	165
How 4: Being a Big Ü	167
Energy 1: Being of service	169
Energy 2: Leaving breadcrumbs	171
Energy 3: Becoming a conduit	173
Energy 4: Always open	175
Key Takeaways	177
Companion Meditation: Reaching Oneness	177
Questions To Ponder	177
The Path Ahead	181
About Laurence	187
About Tom	189
Next Steps	191

THE BIG Ü

Foreword

I FIRST MET Laurence Udell over fifteen years ago. I'd heard about him and his reputation from a close business colleague. At first I thought he was just another consultant, someone to help bring a newly formed team together. What I discovered was that he was something so different and so much more. He turned out to be someone who helped me to get to the core of what I am and wanted to be. He got me to connect in with my soul. He was just what I was looking for as an advisor, business mentor, coach and confidante.

At the time, I was what you would think of as the epitome of a successful businessman, someone really 'on their game'. I had taken over the role of CEO of a struggling business which I turned around and grew to become a successful global business. The shareholders were happy with their returns. I had the support of a loyal team and a happy workforce.

Despite many challenges, setbacks and success and lots of enjoyment, I discovered that the role of a CEO can still be a lonely one and that the buck stopped with me. I am of course no different from many people who, irrespective of their job or responsibility, can feel vulnerable, sometimes overwhelmed, isolated, burdened and just plain unhappy at times.

Laurence brought me back to my centre and reminded me of my reason to be. I made subtle internal shifts and adjustments and my world changed for the better. I feel I have finally found the real me, my Big Ü. Like everyone else, I am a work in progress and still on my own personal journey but I feel more comfortable in my own skin. I now feel better equipped and more focused on what creates the success for me.

Along the way, Laurence encouraged me to start meditating. He introduced me to Tom Evans who helped me get a breakthrough with my meditation. I had always wanted to mediate but quite frankly I had found it hard to switch off and make my overactive mind go quiet. I have learned meditation is not about having no thoughts at all but all about forming a different relationship with my inner chatter. I now try to meditate every day and it brings so many benefits. I quickly learned I got the ten minutes or so I invested each morning back many times over. When I start the day calmly, all those around me seemed to be calm, too. My Big Ü seemed to be getting even bigger.

Through my journey there is not only renewed energy and fire for my role in my business but also in my family life, I am a better husband, son, father and friend to those around me. I have focus, drive and feel awake to the possibilities and opportunities ahead of me. I have greater meaning and purpose in the life I choose to live. The overall effect of my transition means that I now feel life is not happening around me but that I am now making my life happen.

I'm so glad this book has come into existence as it will help many others step into a new world and a new way of life.

Nick Bentley
President, Chief Executive Officer
The RiverStone Group
A Fairfax Company

THE BIG U

About this book

THIS BOOK IS mindfully small in size, while also being large in scope. It is a call to all people who are acting as a small ü yet who harbour an inner calling for their Big Ü to be seen, to be heard and to be counted. As such, it is designed to empower people to live to up to their full potential.

When our small ü is in operation, we can be quite effective but our performance is linear. What we put in, we get out. This is hard work and eventually wears us down. It's like wading through treacle and pushing water uphill.

When our Big Ü comes out to play, we deliver exponential performance. We become more effective, have far greater impact and, at the same time, life becomes easier.

So this book is a response to that calling. It is a call to discover our place of quiet power. From this place, we lead by example, we co-create with ease, flowing and moving through life with grace. When we engage with others, they in turn feel compelled to step up to also become their Big Ü.

This calling requires us to wake up and explore the depths of our heart and soul. It's a call to awaken, to wake up to a new and easier way of being. At the same time, it's a call to wake up to your true meaning, passion and purpose. You end up stepping into and owning your magnificence, your full power and evolve into being the very best version of yourself.

This calling is both intimate and elusive. It doesn't belong to our mind, it belongs to our deepest core – our essence, which is often referred to as our soul. Initially we hear and respond to the calling when both our conscious mind is still and when our body is still. With the silence that comes, our soul appears and becomes truly embodied.

People often overlook this calling as they rush around responding only to external events. As a result they become busy getting things done, building to-do lists and even worrying about what might happen about things that may never happen. We can feel guilty if we are not doing things, although we may not like to admit it. We can be frightened of being still and being with ourselves – alone with solely our mind, our body and our feelings. It can be unnerving to be alone with nobody but ourselves.

It's a place where all the various threads of our lives interweave together to create a golden thread.

Success by other means

We often measure our successes by our performance in the outer world, by the size of our house, the achievements of our children, the registration plate of our car and our job title. Rarely do we assess our level of success by how happy we are, how good our relationships are and how healthy we are. Yet these are the real tangibles of how well we have managed and lived our way through life.

Without a connection to our essence, we unknowingly are depriving ourselves of the love, the freedom, the happiness and the peace which we actually desire and seek. We look outside ourselves trying to be convinced that 'once I do this', 'once I have got that' and 'when this happens', I will be happy and at peace. This cause and effect thinking looks solely to the outer world for the sources of happiness and fulfilment.

This frenetic outer world vanishes when we are meditating, daydreaming or sleeping. These special times allow us to be still and it is then that our innermost core can speak to us. When we discover our essence and connect and align with our soul, it helps us to find our meaning, passion and purpose. This helps us to develop and exponentially grow and transform our lives

– and the lives of others.

It is here our greatness, the very best version of ourselves, our Big Ü, is waiting to be remembered and discovered. When we allow our Big Ü to step forward, it scales everything up. Individually we live the life we love, we are both successful with all that we do and fulfilled at the same time.

Others around us will ask why we are so lucky and how we always land on our feet. We will find others want to awaken their Big Ü, too, and we are not threatened by this, as such an approach scales and multiplies. A business full of Big Ü's is not a collection of Big Egos. The Big Ü organisation is aligned, clear and transparent. Everybody knows its vision, purpose, goals and performance criteria. Everybody knows how they play their part and the alignment they have with their own purpose, goals and criteria. The organisation is adaptive, creative, innovative, lean, smart, will-do and change making, where everyone plays to their strengths, makes a difference and respects the talents of others.

This book is designed to lead you to this place. A place of meaningful success and fulfilment. When you get to the end of this book, you will have discovered more about your essence – you will have made a soul connection. Do not be alarmed that this is a religious conversion by subterfuge, it is an awakening of consciousness.

Each part of this book is designed to help you awaken to the next level of consciousness. As you travel and embrace the road of your truth through this book, you will discover how the four distinct layers can fuse into the one that they first separated and crystallised from.

When we step up and own our Big Ü, struggle becomes a faint memory. Clarity, passion, desire and the fire in our belly fuels us to make the most of everything. Our Big Ü is unstoppable, unflappable, unwavering and unified.

How this book is structured

This book is structured to mirror our four layers of our consciousness, which are nested within each other, rather like Russian dolls. Each of the four parts of this book could easily be expanded to fill a whole book of its own, in a quadrilogy. As they are four parts of a whole, we were keen that they should come together in one small and accessible book.

When you get to the end of this book, you will discover that the innermost layer can be thought of as the outermost layer – and vice versa. These layers are inextricably interwoven, each feeding from and leading to each other. This is a journey of discovery as to how they are entwined.

The four parts of this book are structured identically, as it is our aim to make this awakening easy to follow and easy to implement.

The first part of the book explores the Material World. This is the layer of reality that is most real to us.

The second part of the book describes the Duality of the world in which we live. As we grow, we learn that the world is full of disparity. We live in a world where 1 billion people are hungry and the same number are obese. It sometimes seems that we can't experience the good without being tinged with a little of the bad.

This leads us to the third part of the book, Superconsciousness. Under, around, above and below us, and inside each of the molecules that makes us, there is a higher and connected consciousness which underpins and overarches everything.

The fourth part of the book describes the Oneness of which we all are a part. You will learn how Superconsciousness acts as the glue that holds everything together and brings us to Oneness. When we are born, it is as if we are born into separation so that we can rediscover everything is as one.

The realisation, and embodiment, that everything is connected is what allows the Big Ü to truly step forward and on to the straight road of truth.

In each part you will find:

- ❖ some explanatory thoughts
- ❖ four reasons why you should make the shift
- ❖ four mechanisms of the how
- ❖ four energies to embrace to take you to the next level

Reasons why

Having a 'why' is critical. It gives us direction and the impetus to break through any barriers. It gives us a meaning, passion and purpose and helps us to get up in the morning. It provides a context for all that we do. It gives us a reason to go that extra mile as well as to make subtle changes in order to discover a more delightful way to be.

Mechanics of how

When it comes to any 'hows', we want them to be as simple and doable as possible. None of them in this book are beyond reach. Doing some of the hows may feel strange, counter-intuitive and as if we are walking against the grain. This is because you will be breaking down old barriers, beliefs, programmes and conditioning. This is evidence change is happening. The hows design in this book is such that, with daily repetition, they become second nature: your way of being and doing. They are the building blocks of your Big Ü.

Energies to embrace

The energies in each part act as precursors to prepare you to smoothly enter the next level. They allow you to tap into your core essence and the depths of your soul. When we allow our soul to take the lead, feelings and knowings align with new, unlimited thoughts and ideas, which then drive our actions and behaviours. To help tap into these energies, each part of this book is also accompanied by a guided meditation to help you awaken the qualities required to move to the next level. At all times, note that you will be taking charge of your progress.

Each chapter ends with some key takeaways and some questions to ponder before moving on.

Caveats

This book models real life on many levels. The messages, words, energies, experiences, ideas and approaches in this book have been born and supported by a mix of neuroscience, the sciences of the psyche and body, and the authors' experiences of living conscious and practical lives.

They are underpinned by many sources of ageless wisdom. They work; they make a difference. They provide the straight road to the truth.

This book, though, comes with four caveats.

Caveat 1

When you find your Big Ü, the little, old ü comes along for the ride. The baby does not get thrown out with the bathwater. The grit that was in the oyster creates a shining pearl. Indeed, when we learn how to access all four levels of consciousness at once, and at will, the world becomes our oyster – we come home.

Caveat 2

You can also discover your Big Ü in stages. Some will be comfortable to awaken to a quarter, a half or three quarters of the way. You can take the journey as fast or as slowly as you like. Some will want to go the whole way and will be led to ask if there are more steps still. There are!

Caveat 3

There is no need to join a cult or change your religion. This book builds on, and augments, your starting position. It is agnostic and complementary to both those who are secular and those of faith.

Caveat 4

This is not an academic textbook. You must have fun on the way. A good indicator that there is a better way is if the fun disappears from the process at any time. Find the joy and you will find the value and the path. You take charge of the journey at all times.

Time to awaken

There is a belief in some circles that awakening requires us to experience a trauma or a crisis such as a life-threatening illness or accident, the loss of a loved one, the loss of meaning and purpose, redundancy or depression. Such events do get us to go deep into ourselves, to question our identity and to ask deeper, more meaningful questions. We are right to ask questions like 'what is life all about' and 'who am I'?

There is a simpler, less traumatic path to awakening that doesn't necessarily mean we have to go to hell and back. By understanding the whys and the hows and embracing the energies in this book, you can awaken safely and joyfully.

When we are asleep and dreaming, we are not aware of our awakened state. When we are awake, we can recognise somebody sleeping is less aware than we are. This brings us to the crux of this book.

What actually happens when you wake up?

Let your Big Ü show you.

ABOUT THIS BOOK

THE BIG Ü

Companion Meditations

THE DISCOVERY OF your Big Ü is something to be experienced. It happens in a series of gentle stages interspersed with huge leaps in understanding and flashes of enlightenment.

To help you on your path, we have recorded four special guided meditations. They are each exactly, and mindfully, 14 minutes 44 seconds long. They are ideal for new and experienced meditators alike.

They are designed to awaken the energies in each part of the book. You can listen to them before each part, during each part or after reading each part.

We strongly recommend you listen to each of them at least once before moving on to the next section. You will also find that some of the answers to the questions to ponder at the end of each part might come along.

We recommend you don't listen to them while driving or operating machinery, as they may well make you sleepy.

Indeed, if you do drop off while listening to them, remarkably and bizarrely, they still work.

The meditations are:

- ❖ Part 1: Being Grounded
- ❖ Part 2: Whole Mind Harmonisation
- ❖ Part 3: Accessing Superconsciousness
- ❖ Part 4: Reaching Oneness

Find out how to get access to the meditations here:

http://thebigu.me/companion-meditations

Journaling

When reading this book and listening to these guided meditations, it can be beneficial to keep a gratitude journal where you document the good things that happen in your life. You can also keep a record of your feelings and reactions as you read the book and listen to the meditations. Be sure to make special note of any coincidences, serendipities and opportunities that come your way, as these are a sign you are finding your path.

Part One
The Material World

'The real voyage of discovery consists not in seeking new lands but in seeing with new eyes.'

Proust

The Material World

WE ARE ALL incredibly lucky to be alive. Our ability to write this book, and your ability to read or listen to it, is nothing short of wondrous and miraculous.

Our planet orbits around a star that has been benign and stable enough, for long enough, for life to evolve and for some of it to achieve a level of self-awareness. We sometimes think of humans as being the only self-aware life forms on Earth but it is worth taking note that many primates, cetaceans, cephalopods and even magpies can recognise themselves in a mirror.

As you will see in this book, there are many levels of awareness. Observe a sleeping baby for one example. Google the 'octopus opening a jar' video for another.

The Goldilocks Zone

All life on Earth comes about as our planet sits in the so-called 'Goldilocks zone'. It is not too hot and not too cold. Our planet revolves on its axis once a day to ensure all parts of the planet get about the same amount sunlight at some time or other over the seasons. With days as long as their year, Venusians do not have this luxury. Martian nights are nearly 100 degrees centigrade colder than their days.

Our planet's gravity is just strong enough to ensure that the atmosphere doesn't escape into space. Venus has too much of the wrong type of atmosphere and Mars has too little. We are able to breathe.

Most of us are strong enough that we can lift our legs and move around unaided. We are smart enough to build machines that propel us around and even escape earthly bonds completely. If our legs fail us, we are clever enough to create machines that can wheel us around. If such machines are not self-propelled or motorised, other humans are often kind enough to push the differently-abled around.

The universe that we inhabit, which allows our solar system to exist in the first place, has just the right conditions for matter to exist. The masses and characteristics of atomic and subatomic particles are 'just right'.

Our three-dimensional universe also incorporates another useful dimension. It follows the forward arrow of time. This is convenient as it means that everything doesn't happen at once. We can take our time to take it all in, to plan, to experience, to learn and to grow.

Despite all this wonderment, and the amazing happenstances that have led to us having the experience of being alive, many people can feel entrapped by these dimensions. The forward arrow of time means our lives will come to an end. We are confined to a physical body that will eventually succumb to the ravages of time.

In our modern world, we are also one of more than 7 billion people trying to make their way in life. With such inherent restrictions, it is tempting to stay small, to play it safe and to avoid rocking the boat. Why should we attempt to be a Big Ü in a world where we are such a very small cog?

Virtually everyone alive now will be a memory in 100 years anyway. With such finite limitations, why should we bother?

After all, it appears that we are thrust into this four-dimensional world without a choice, with a pre-dealt deck of cards. Some of us have had childhoods where we were cherished and loved. Some of us may have been neglected or even abused, perhaps shut away not to be thought of or spoken about ever again. Throughout our life we have experiences that can impact us physically, mentally and emotionally. All of this conditions us to how we behave and perform in this world now.

Certain people have the ability to get us worked up, to touch our hot points and to trigger us to react and behave in a certain way. Our environment, too, can have a big impact on our behaviour and performance. Some people struggle to balance work life and home life, where they have two different personas. This is a difficult act to pull off.

Stop the world, I want to get off

In our Material World, we seem to be relentlessly pursuing advancement and progression with smarter, always-on technology and so-called artificial intelligence. Nowadays we are all broadcasters, or narrowcasters at least, as everybody can have their say and have it heard all around the world. Expectations and demands go through the roof. Everybody wants more and more.

Some people need to show others what they have got in order to justify their existence, saying things like:

'I have a good standing and place in this world.'

'I am successful.'

'I can take more selfies than you.'

Yet with all of this has come greater challenges for both us as the human race and us as individuals. People are putting up greater barriers to protect what they consider is their own. Wars are rife, competition is fierce. Fear and anxiety is commonplace.

Depressed parents are depressing their children, so growing numbers of teenagers become afflicted too. We have even created labels such as 'social media depression' and 'generation snowflake'. The latter is a neologism used to characterise millennials as being more prone to taking offence than previous generations, or as being too emotionally vulnerable to cope with views that challenge their own.

This thinking is unhelpful and derogatory as it deflects blame on to the afflicted. It is a distortion of perspective that ignores the fact that each generation brings something new. Challenging of the old ways leads to the creation of new ways. Without this, we wouldn't have survival of the human race and we wouldn't evolve. While our ability to create new technology has progressed, what is now lagging behind is our development of a 'technology' for the spirit, mind, heart, soul and body.

Behind the mask

Everybody at their core wants to be loved, to feel safe, to be happy and to be seen for who and what they are. Yet when masks are worn, things are left unsaid and true feelings are unexpressed. By doing so, the hope is often that we will be accepted and acceptable. This leads to misalignment between our thoughts and our deeds which creates a gap for our small ü to reign supreme.

The donning of a mask is a viable coping strategy, just for a while. After all some have even been worn since childhood. Masks help us to survive in the here and now. We try to convince others, and ourselves, that we are happy and contented with what we have. Ultimately this impacts on us personally. It drains us of our energy, our hopes and desires. It stops us speaking our truths. It closes our hearts and access to our soul.

We can become dead from the inside out, which stops us from trusting, loving and thinking for ourselves. As a result, we find ourselves lost and in fear. We strive for greater control and it always seems to be just out of our reach.

When we run our lives from a materialistic perspective, from the outside in, life becomes hard and we believe we need to run faster just to stand still. When you live your life from the inside out, which at first requires some bravery, life becomes a breeze. The usual 'fight, flight or freeze' behaviour, which is hardwired into our lower brainstem, gets replaced by the 'stay, play and sway' tendency of our heart mind.

If we keep our head down, nobody can hurt us, so why should we bother? Why should we do anything? Surely it is down to someone else?

Why 1: It's easier

So one of the telltale signs we are allowing our small ü to predominate is that life becomes somewhat of a struggle. What we seek feels as if it is just around the corner. We often see, sense and even touch opportunities that will deliver our wildest dreams. Yet getting to where we'd like to be forever, feels somewhat intangible. External events get in the way. Time and money are often used as scapegoats, as are the government, Brexit, rogue presidents and Lady Luck. The glass is perpetually half empty and nowhere nearing half full.

When we step into our Big Ü, that same glass is perpetually over-brimming and self-filling. Opportunity visits our door daily and serendipity shows up around every corner. What's more, nothing has to materially change in our Material World. It all comes from a change in mindset, or more specifically mind-sets and heart-sets. It involves us allowing feelings and emotions to come to the surface so we can discover our essence and expose the core of who we really are.

When we wake up and raise our consciousness, adversity merely offers opportunity. If we hit a rocky patch, the Big Ü sees it as an area for growth, learning and transformation. Once our

Big Ü embraces and takes the learning on board, we are better placed to help others similarly afflicted.

A Big Ü also takes guidance from adversity. While others might be dismayed, or think they have failed in some way, when we hit a brick wall, the Big Ü takes it as a sign. There might be an easier way. The timing might not be optimal. A bigger and even better opportunity may be lurking just around the corner. The Big Ü knows to take one step backwards, three sideways, to wait for a couple of revolutions of the Earth, or orbits of the moon, before stepping forward again. The solution will reveal itself.

The Big Ü is the vehicle for our essence, our soul. It lives by our innate wisdom and knows our truth. It is connected to all that is and is rooted in love not fear. It is more natural to just be who we are, trust in ourselves, speak our truth and be happy to be seen for who we truly are. This is us at our core and not necessarily the personality that has been conditioned over the years, or the behaviours that we have adopted from our parents or guardians. These patterns have become embedded in us, creating our being.

From an evolutionary perspective, the primitive parts of our brain generate our baseline behaviours of fight, flight or freeze. In time gone by, this was vital for survival. In many cases in our modern world, it serves us well if we can elevate ourselves to respond in a more mindful manner.

When we allow these base instincts to dominate, it keeps us in the default position of our small ü. This response should not be disparaged or ignored as it can literally be a lifesaver in some circumstances. There are other base-level responses to be considered, too. Our need to be loved, and to feel secure, also drives many of our behaviours.

To make the most of our lives, to feel free and to step into our full power, we must consciously rewire ourselves. This requires us to form a new relationship with these base-level feelings and emotions. Initially, this can feel counter-intuitive.

When we awaken, however, we discover a new why, when life takes on a new level of engagement, interaction and even excitement. The Big Ü is pure, simple and easy.

Why 2: The time is now

The pendulum is swinging towards a time of higher awareness for all humankind. Fortunately many of the younger generation already understand and are aware of this shift. Some are struggling to operate in this world, with many of the older generation still being in positions of power and authority.

The world around us has transformed beyond recognition in recent decades. The older generations are all in danger of being left behind if they don't start retraining and realigning themselves.

There are significant changes in society and in the way we conduct business. Winds of change are blowing through politics, commerce and how we care for the environment. Unfortunately, but perhaps understandably, many of those in positions of authority are reluctant to accept change, fearing that they might lose that power they have struggled for so long to attain. They are becoming aware that the old way of doing things is no longer the answer but they don't know how to behave differently. They are perhaps quietly worried, in fear and grasping to hold on, even though they often don't admit it. They must stop the struggle; let go of the very thing that is holding them back. They should adapt their behaviour and understand that their roles will soon be taken over by the younger generation.

We need to transform the way we use our brains and remember how to connect with our hearts and souls if we are to keep up with the world we have created. This will help us steer ourselves to the next level of success and fulfilment.

This is mankind's golden opportunity to make everything better by a quantum leap and each of us can contribute to by waking up to another level. We may currently feel lost, empty, the struggle is too hard, as if something is missing or there must be more than this. Well yes, it can all be different, better, happier, more fulfilling, for individuals and as a species. The good news and opportunity is that the changes and transformations are best started at an individual, personal level.

Something remarkable happens when we adopt responsibility for our personal transformation. We are shown the straight line to our truth. We step on to a path known as the golden thread, where we get pulled towards our own place of egoless, and soul-lead, magnificence.

The future success of mankind lies in our own hands and the aim of this book is to help awaken those leaders within us to help speed up the growth and transformation of our species. To do this, we believe we can tap into and blend together the age-old Eastern spiritual wisdoms, such as Buddhism, Shamanism and Sufism with traditional, analytical Western thinking. At the same time, we can embrace the latest scientific discoveries from quantum physics and neuroscience. The aim is to deliver tangible, real-life, practical benefits across our society, in the environment, in politics and in commerce.

It is an urban myth that our brains are still hardwired the same way they have been for millennia. In times gone by, when we were hunter-gatherers, farmers, settlers and even industrialists, this wiring served us well.

Now we are living in an age of knowledge where we are increasingly utilising so-called artificial intelligence. The moment of singularity is imminently approaching, when the many technologies come together and surpass our human abilities.

There is another singularity which is much closer to home and perhaps more imminent. This, perhaps more realisable, singularity is the synthesis of our spirit, mind, heart, soul and body. When we allow this singularity to unfold, artificial intelligence is not a threat but an ally. It is also not really artificial but an emulation and augmentation of natural processes.

Why 3: It opens new doors

You will have heard it said that the same thinking yields the same results. What goes on inside our heads is mirrored in the Material World and what we notice about the Material World creates our sense of reality.

It has also been said that truth is a mere reflection of how what we perceive fits our model of the world. By changing our perception, our reality therefore changes. By extending and augmenting our perception, our world expands in proportion.

The traditionally recognised five senses we use to survey the Material World can all be honed and developed. Each of us can learn how to train our ears so that we can play a musical instrument, or just appreciate others playing and singing. Likewise, each of us can become an artist, a perfumer, a sommelier and a massage therapist and further develop our senses of sight, smell, taste and touch as a result. In developing these senses, new doors will open, too.

Neuroscientists are fast realising that we have vastly more senses than this. The mystic Rudolph Steiner referred to these as super-sensibilities. We can sense the mood when we come into a room. We can 'smell' a business opportunity and 'see' our way into the future.

When writing a book like this, the words come through the authors, not from them.

Navigating the world merely using the traditional senses is like looking at it through a letterbox, with cataracts. When we awaken to our fully alive senses and sensibilities, the door gets flung wide open to allow us to step into a new world.

Our brains are not just generators of thought but receivers of thought forms too. Some thought forms percolate up from our 'lower' mind centres. These unconscious murmurs from our gut and heart minds often get overruled by the loud inner chatter of our brain. When we learn their signature and heed their guidance, we will rarely put a foot wrong. If you have ever not followed your gut or not listened when your heart wasn't in it, you will know what we mean.

The awakening of our Big Ü requires that we learn a new language and start a new dialogue with these mind centres. We can use them as our internal satnav.

It is now known that our gut contains more neurons than a cat's brain and we are only hungry when 'it' is hungry. It also senses danger and gives us a sense of right and wrong. Likewise, it used to be thought our heart was controlled from our head. It, too, is an independent mind and self-governs. It also seeks love and gives love. It truly is the heart of who we are. When we work and operate in environments that we love, where we are loved and respected for who and what we are, our hearts literally radiate soul warmth and ignite our Big Ü.

There are other thought forms that come from the top of our head and the back of our mind. These are somewhat ethereal and come in sometimes when we are least expecting them – sometimes when we are driving, even going the loo or in the shower. It pays dividends to listen to such aha moments as they can open even wider doors for us. In igniting our Big Ü, we are opening the door to cross a new threshold where we get to see a fuller picture and a wider perspective from many angles.

In less than a second, we are all capable of having a thought that can change our world and the world at large. This could be one thought that brings greater opportunities and infinite possibilities, as one change leads to another.

Why 4: It scales

The integration and harmonisation of our mind centres, and recognition that all thoughts are not necessarily what we can call our own, has scalability.

When we have internal harmony, it leads to external harmony with those around us. People sense our passion and that we are on a mission not solely driven by ego. When people see we are getting results and making waves by stepping into a mode called quiet power, they want to know the secret. We become nicely infectious.

The organ that leads the way in creating our own internal and group harmony is our heart. Its electromagnetic field can be detected many metres away from our body and it is much stronger than the field generated by our heads. When a team of people are all in love with what they do, they operate cohesively and the whole becomes bigger than the sum of the parts.

When we open our hearts and connect with others from our hearts, love flows to and from us. Greater connections are made, more meaningful relationships are created. Our actions, interactions and performances become transformational, rather than transactional. We become more curious, flexible, engaging, aligned and open. We look for opportunities for co-creation, rather than seeking to blame, criticise or judge. We take a lead bringing joy and excitement into a toxic environment. We search for possibilities and how we can work around adversity. This is a place where the Big Ü feels at home.

It only takes one bad apple, or naysayer, to disrupt that collective field. Turning such naysayers into 'yaysayers' is not something to do by dominance but by understanding their perspectives with compassion. It is prudent to discover what would have to change to turn their 'nays' into 'yays'. This works well in small teams as well as in the wider organisation, and even in international negotiations.

Success breeds success. People at peace with themselves radiate that peace to others. Being the Big Ü brings out the best in others as they don't see you as a threat. They find that they don't need to be careful, on high alert for danger or to play it small and not be seen. They know their meaning and purpose. They, too, naturally start to show up by being themselves, wanting to be seen and really wanting to make a difference.

You will find that they want to contribute and add value to the task in hand, those around them and the bigger goals. They start to bathe in the feelings and emotions of joy, excitement, passion and commitment that flow from us. Our

Big Ü paves the way for other Big Ü's to stand up and become present.

Hearts and minds grow, expand and transform and ultimately can get to a place where there is no beginning and no end, where everything is possible. Everybody and everything benefits exponentially. Everything is magnified as one change leads to another.

The scaling up, from stepping into your Big Ü, is limitless in both time and space. As you will see, your growth and personal development augments the collective consciousness of all humankind, and all other life forms. You don't need to be an author, teacher or have progeny for your learnings to be passed on for future generations.

It may be somewhat apocryphal but when 100 monkeys on one island learn to use a twig to extract honey, others on neighbouring islands, with no direct communication, start to do it, too.

The mechanisms for such transfer are well known in metaphysical circles. It is our hope and aim that this century will see them being fully understood and embraced by 'mainstream science'.

How 1: Take responsibility

In the same way nobody can breathe for you, eat for you or love for you, you are the only person to elect to awaken to your Big Ü. You are the only person to decide how big you want your Big Ü to get. You are solely responsible for the speed, scope and nature of your journey.

It is vital to take full responsibility, and nothing less than 100 per cent commitment is required. We become the sole arbiters of our actions, our thought processes and the way we want to feel and to be. We cannot blame circumstances, other people or situations for what is not going our way. It requires taking total ownership for all that is in our lives.

When we take full responsibility, we remove all excuses for things not going our way. We gain a new understanding of the limiting beliefs and distracting behaviours that we have developed over our lifetime. We see that they have only served to keep us small, and safe.

This new perspective allows us to consciously retract into the safe shell of our small ü when we need to, perhaps for tactical reasons. Our Big Ü can then step out initially in situations where it is safe.

Something remarkable happens when we become mindful of our impact. Our Big Ü steps forward and replaces our smaller ü.

We come to a realisation that it was our own behaviours and reactions that were instrumental in maintaining the old status quo.

All journeys of this nature require us to be bold and to have courage while being compassionate and gentle with ourselves. Taking responsibility in this way does not mean we give ourselves a hard time. We should also take responsibility for being gentle on ourselves.

How 2: Be honest and authentic

Like all the aspects of the awakening journey, honesty, truthfulness and authenticity manifests in two forms – internally to ourselves and externally to others.

Any awakening is dual in nature and must only be for our betterment and not to the detriment of others. Ideally, seek the win–win. Ask yourself how your awakening can be for mutual benefit of all.

Being honest, truthful and authentic requires that we question our motives regularly. Actions carry more weight than mere declarations of intent. Be wary of those who feel they must declare their honesty. Empty vessels often make the loudest noise after all.

It is difficult at first but we have to become honest about our internal thoughts and to be truthful about our motivations and drivers. In this regard, it helps to 'go meta', or above and beyond, with our goals. So once a goal is defined, think about where it might lead you once it is realised. When that higher goal is then achieved, ask where this might lead in turn. This is how we can discover our real motive.

Once this motive is discovered, we can begin to be truly authentic externally. This is the first step in showing the world what our Big Ü is capable of and all about – through our quiet power – where we don't force it on any one, we are just present.

When our Big Ü begins to operate, it is the precursor to an even Bigger Ü showing up. We are shown what is true and how to be true. This helps us to steer a true path.

Consistency in thought and action allows us to maintain an authentic presence. People around us know we can be trusted and rest easy in the knowledge that we are coming from a good place.

How 3: Belief and trust

We are often our own biggest critic and biggest doubter. This can be especially so when we undertake any transformation or personal development. For starters, we can quickly forget what it was like to be our former smaller ü, as the new version of us becomes active. We can sometimes think perhaps that everything is just the same and that we are imagining it.

Fortunately the interconnections between our neurons are 'plastic'. Just by thinking differently, we rewire our brain and our neurology. So, if we believe we can change, we can. If we think the cards we are dealt with are fixed, or even rigged, they are!

Of course, it helps if we can have a little proof. The best way to establish if there is any change is by becoming mindful of external events. When we first awaken, we can be challenged with adversity and be blessed by opportunity.

Should any such adversity visit your door, notice that when your reaction to it changes, it doesn't seem to revisit. Conversely, if we react the same way as we always do, we will find that it keeps coming back to haunt us.

When opportunity graces our path, it can also be a test to check how we react. If we are used to jumping into situations with both feet, they can prove to be false dawns and end up with the adverse consequence of being disappointing. On the other hand, opportunities will appear that are effortless as they play to your natural strengths.

It takes time for our self-belief to grow and for us to trust we are on the right path. Wandering off the path is the only way to find it again.

By taking small steps and testing the water, the gap between where we were and where we want to be narrows. We then realise that we have been 'a-voiding' this particular void.

How 4: Take action

When we make a commitment, it requires willingness to give our time and energy to something we believe in. We make a promise and firm decision to do something or other. We rule out all other options and throw ourselves wholly at our stated action and do it. All our hopes and dreams come to nought if we take no action.

The first action in any journey of change and personal transformation is to take some time out. Before embarking on the day, or picking up a new task, pause and slow your breathing down. At least once a day, take time out to do some physical activity, maybe just take a walk in nature.

Each week at least, extend your consciousness and learn something new. For example, by reading this book, or any book for that matter, you have already augmented your awareness.

If you find that first step forward a little daunting, there are a couple of tricks you can pull. First, you can take a few steps sideways until you see an opening for you to move ahead. Second, it is sometimes tactical to take a step or two backwards. If this latter course of action is the only way, for every step you take backwards, make sure you take at least two forwards.

As you continue on this journey, you will also learn that mindfully taking no action is often as good as, or even better than, taking action just for the sake of it. Sometimes it simply isn't the ideal time to take a step forward and there can be a more optimal date, or set of circumstances, to set a ball in motion.

If you always do what you have always done, you will always get what you have always got. If you want to get somewhere different, then you have to do something you have not done before.

Energy 1: Observing and witnessing

When we do create ripples in the pond of life, it pays great dividends to observe how they spread out. Some of them will reach the metaphorical shoreline and bounce back towards us. If we are always making a splash, we might miss these subtle returns.

The key to developing your Big Ü lies in observing and witnessing your impact in the world and in noticing the changes in the world within you and around you. Observing yourself, and others, without being critical or judgemental is the key. You will discover the delight of observing how your words, actions and behaviours help others.

Here it is key that we witness without value judgements but with compassion and empathy. From this place we see a bigger, fuller picture. We see the full context of any situation. We get the opportunity to decide, ideally from our heart, how we wish to be proactive and not just reactive.

When observing ourselves and witnessing how we think, act, feel and behave, we must also be mindful to discover our shadow. Our shadow consciousness is where our deepest secrets are both consciously and unconsciously hidden. The key to becoming an excellent observer of the traits of our shadow lies in maintaining a quiet mind. The key to making our mind go quiet lies in meditating daily.

Meditation is not about having no thoughts at all but in having a different relationship with your thoughts. As the normal human mind can only experience one thought at a time, if we mull over the past or worry about the future, we will lose focus on what we are doing right now and what is going on around us.

If we treat ourselves to just ten minutes of mindful meditation every day, our mind is quieter during the day and less prone to wander. As a result, we quickly become better observers.

Energy 2: Courage and curiosity

A Big Ü is not a big ego, in the classic sense. A Big Ü does indeed have a heightened sense of self, which is the connection with the Big Heart. Coming from your heart you are open, respectful and mindful of others. The Big Ü is passionate about continuously learning.

Learning a new skill can take some courage. Thoughts of our childhood and exams come to the surface. We may worry about not being so good at it, or failing. The best way not to fail is to not even try.

We can learn in many ways. Traditionally we use education and training to extend our knowledge and our skills. By far the best way, though, is to learn through discovery and practice. This plays to the natural ability and predisposition of the two hemispheres of our brain.

In most people, the right brain looks at the big picture and deals with the embracing of new situations. The left brain focuses on detail and processes learned responses. When we engage both hemispheres in the learning process, the cautious left brain starts to see the benefit of 'thinking big'. The right brain gets encouraged by the left brain's acceptance and becomes more and more curious.

Incidentally any model of how the left and right brains work is merely a model and simplistic generalisation, but intuitively your Big Ü will see the sense and benefit of the metaphor. Learning through discovery becomes part of everyday life.

By being courageously curious, we begin to see the patterns in our life and the behaviours that have created them. We can then can make new and better choices in what we want to keep and what we want to release. Such curiosity guides us into the flow of life and into a magical zone where the impossible becomes the possible.

Energy 3: Sensitivity

As we become more curious, we become more sensitive to how what we think, feel and do impacts the world around us. As such, one of the aims for your Big Ü is to be sensitive to the egos of others and the true nature of your own ego.

We should be sensitive to the two aspects of ego – that which is shown and that which remains in the shadow. The part of ego we know gives us the sense of us. It is who we are, or who we think we are.

The shadow ego is the part of our psyche that is trying to keep us safe, so it doesn't like change or anything that is unfamiliar. It is the voice in your head warning you that if you change you run the risk of losing everything.

One aspect of the shadow ego is that it tells us that we are better than everyone else and have all the answers. It is driven to this delusion by fear. It makes us believe that we've got to be better than others in order to protect ourselves from them. It makes us competitive and jealous and envious. It makes us defensive and reactive.

Being sensitive of ego is not a weakness, it is a strength. It requires that we connect with ourselves in a more subtle manner. We should be more compassionate and open with our emotions and about how we are feeling.

When we are honest with others about our vulnerabilities, it allows us to converse and explore at a deeper level.

Our egos make ripples in the pond by the mere fact that we are alive. Thought alone creates these ripples. Being sensitive to the content and the nature of our thought forms is as important for a Big Ü as being mindful of our speech and actions.

Energy 4: Daring greatly

In some ways this book is a dare. We are daring you to step up into a new way of being and doing and then to discover what happens when you do. Our main motivation is that both we, and our clients, have experienced that life gets easier when we step up. We want to share the benefits, to all and sundry, of a more graceful and less stressful way of being.

This book is not daring you in the same way children might dare others to do something naughty, or to break the rules. Although you may at times feel something isn't quite right, as making the changes to our habits and conditioning can feel counter-intuitive. We are daring you to become more caring, for both yourself and others. A Big Ü dares to be different.

The book is daring you to break the mould and to become disruptive of old ways that don't serve you any longer. We are daring you to show up, to be seen and to step into your own greatness by letting your small ü be replaced by your Big Ü.

Rather than thinking 'he who dares wins', be mindful that 'she who dares grins'. When we take on a dare and deliver upon it, we can quite rightly smile internally that we've moved up a gear.

While this book is a dare, it is important to

know where the dares really emanate from.

Our soul knows our path and what is good for us. Your soul helped you to find this book, and all other circumstances during your life, to help you evolve to the biggest and best version of Ü.

Once you are open to be led by your soul, you become lucky in life. You become able to make possible what was previously improbable and seemed impossible. We dare you to do it.

KEY TAKEAWAYS

The Material World is very real.
It is also the tip of a very large iceberg.
The cards we are dealt with can be exchanged.
We are solely responsible for all that unfolds in our lives.

COMPANION MEDITATION: BEING GROUNDED

This first meditation is a guided visualisation that leads the listener to a new understanding of our three dimensional world. It forms a new bond with the Material World which keeps you safe and grounded for the journey ahead.

QUESTIONS TO PONDER

What will you not settle for?
Why are you playing it small?
How would you invest your time if money was no object?
What is the deepest secret you haven't told another human being?

Part Two
Duality

'Just as we have two eyes and two feet, Duality is part of life.'

Carlos Santana

Duality

THERE IS AGE-OLD belief that the road to enlightenment involves experiencing some kind of external trauma, like divorce, bereavement, ill health or redundancy. Some people go right to the edge and back, either through traumatic illness or accident, addiction or life-threatening happenstances.

These types of event cause us to question our whole identity and the very meaning and purpose of our lives. We are brought to ask what is really important to us and what might we need to do in order to change and move forward.

Generally these crises occur in midlife, which is no longer for many in their 40s but in their 50s or even 60s. Such crises are now also increasingly prevalent in the younger generations who, quite rightly, are asking why. Whenever it occurs, it is important that we see through the illusion and awaken to the new reality at a time of our own choosing, rather than waiting for it to be forced upon us by circumstances.

Why wait for a crisis to strike if you can avert it with a few simple and profound changes? There is no particular need to go to hell and back in order to awaken, unless you want to.

It just requires us to make some shifts, create new habits and to look at ourselves and the world through new eyes.

The first shift in thinking requires us to embrace the dual nature of our reality. At a fundamental level, this is something physicists are struggling with. They are pondering whether everything is made of particles, or just distilled from waves of probability. This microcosmic dichotomy scales to the macro level. Every second of every day, we choose between two or more possibilities. We can choose to get something done or to procrastinate. We can see the world as a place where danger lurks or where opportunity lies around every corner.

In two minds

It is perhaps no surprise that we can see the world in two ways as we are all blessed with a brain with in-built asymmetry. One of the reasons we can be in two minds, or more, about something or other is that the two hemispheres of our brain have different experiences of the world.

The idea of a logical left brain and creative

right brain is now seen as somewhat of an urban myth. While still a generalisation, as our brains are plastic and can rewire in an instant, it is better to see our two hemispheres as having different views of the world.

In most people, the left brain primarily sits inside space and time, pays attention to detail and processes learned responses. At the same time, our right brain sits everywhere and 'everywhen' else, embraces and learns the new and looks at the big picture. Armed with this model, you will be able to recognise dreamers who spend days sitting in their right hemispheres, and those left brainers who tick boxes, work from to-do lists and keep track of their expenses daily.

As we awaken to the next level, we will be increasingly comfortable with those with an asymmetric leaning in their consciousness. At the same time, we should be mindful of our own tendencies, while taking steps to synchronise and harmonise our two hemispheres to work together on the same tasks at the same time. Fortunately, the techniques and tricks to do this are both simple and accessible.

The tip of the iceberg

At the same time as the outer cortex of our brain seems to be hardwired to perceive in two ways what we call reality, our mind is also split between conscious and unconscious thoughts, feelings, memories and emotions.

Furthermore, what we are conscious of at any one time is far outweighed by that of which we are unconscious. While the normal human mind can only experience one thought at a time, that one thought pops out at the tip of the iceberg from billions of unconscious thought forms and feelings.

While the language centres in our brain might generate thought patterns like, 'I am not cut out for this' or 'I'm just not good enough', our experience of our world is distributed and encoded in our whole neurology, not just in the neurons in our brain.

We might tap our foot without knowing it or our stomach might tighten with fear and our face might blush if we are asked to stand up and speak in public.

Worries stick in our gut and, if left unchecked, can lead to an irritable bowel. If our heart is broken too many times, it can lead to heart and circulatory dis-ease.

The foundations for these fears and beliefs could have been laid when you were a small child. They might have been instilled through your parents, your peer group, your teachers or your bosses, from a time when you were young and insecure.

From wherever they were instilled, they become an intrinsic part of our nature. We need to explore and understand them if we want to overcome them and become a bigger Ü.

Soul and ego

Our dual nature is not limited to two brain hemispheres or the dual nature of our consciousness. It is said that we are not humans on a spiritual journey but spirits on a human journey. Whether you are religious, agnostic or an atheist, it helps in the awakening process to acknowledge the existence of a soul.

This is the essence of us that 'knows' who we truly are and is cognizant of our mission, purpose and true capability. We stress that there is no need to sign up to a cult or change your beliefs in order to find your Big Ü, but it helps if you run with the idea that we all possess an all-knowing and all-seeing soul.

At the same time, our ego resides in the vehicle of our physical body. Our ego gives us our sense of self and who we are.

There is sometimes a conflict between the ego and the soul because they both have different needs. As babies, we are completely dependent on our parents. As our brains form, we learn that certain behaviours, like crying and smiling, get certain results. We take cues and instructions from our parents, and later our teachers, and modify our behaviours accordingly.

For example, if our parents tell us to be quiet, they are conditioning our behaviour. Our ego might want to keep us safe, so we learn to stay quiet. While this is going on, our ego is developing and learning what we need to do in order to get what we want.

At the same time, our soul silently and gently encourages us to be free and to live more expansively. If the ego and the soul remain disconnected, we can suffer from mental diseases like bipolar disorder and schizophrenia. This is the extreme condition of being in two minds about something or other. Most people have been pulled in more than one direction at some point in their lives.

Once we allow our soul and ego to integrate, we have a much easier ride. Our soul acts as a guide and our ego takes on the multiple role of director, actor and stagehand in the Material World.

At this point, we become a conduit in the Duality. Where previously our dual world was full of paradoxes, perceived conflicts and seen and unseen challenges, it is now that everything starts to make sense.

We see how one and one can make three when

we tap into both male and female energies. We can learn how to create a synthesis from both Eastern and Western philosophies. We see that fear and love both have their place and their role. Our yin and yang fuse into one Big Ü.

Why 1: Hardship is an illusion

It is an illusion that life is intrinsically hard and that the world is out to get us. Our so-called leaders have either consciously or unconsciously capitalised on this misunderstanding down the ages. In the 'new age', leadership is devolved and distributed. Nowadays everyone is capable of leadership and this starts with leading ourselves, before attempting to lead others.

The physical three-dimensional world around us is a projection of consciousness. It is real and unreal at the same time. This is the paradox of being in the Duality. If you hit your thumb with a hammer, it will hurt. Yet the pain induced and sensed by your brain is not real insofar as you can't weigh it or give it to someone else.

In this illusion, thoughts don't so much become things, but they are things. In the next 100 years, new theories will embed consciousness into our physics. It is the large missing part of the universe that has scientists so baffled.

What is so good about this realisation is that you don't have to wait for a scientific theory to explain it all to capitalise upon it. Our brains don't know the difference between reality and visualisation unless we tell them. At one end of the spectrum, you have victims who blame others for everything that happens or doesn't happen to them, but at the other end you have those who create their own reality. They are the ones who make life happen for them rather than allowing life to happen to them.

The power to achieve unimaginably great things is already present within all of us, we just need to give ourselves permission to dream and then to turn those dreams into reality. Unless you are born with a silver spoon in your mouth, you may be wondering how to pay your bills, and are living in survival mode. This is after all how we are hardwired. We end up constantly in the flight or fight mode, unable to tap into our creative spirit and to take advantage of co-creative opportunities.

Our ally in making the transition is the soul. When we meditate, or take a walk in nature, we give our ego an opportunity to rest and to take guidance. This guidance can pop along as an idea or a knowing. Equally, it can come in the form of a sign. If more than one person tells you to read a particular book or an old contact pops up, out of the blue, see this as just what you have been looking for.

You will soon discover that the practice of daily meditation stops being a chore and starts to form a nice-to-have habit. The days you treat yourself to some me time will go much more smoothly than the days you rush at life like a bull in a china shop.

Something much more subtle goes on with meditation than making our mind go quiet. Meditation on the breath energises our neurons and new synaptic connections are formed. We become better at spotting coincidences. Not only do we get more done in less time but the quality of our creative output improves.

We end up in flow and in the zone and all those memories of hardship begin to dissipate. Our dreams and our daydreams begin to merge with our waking thoughts. What were once mere faint wishes, wants and desires start to manifest.

This is one of the most subtle and powerful aspects of allowing your Big Ü to come to the surface. You just dream your wildest dreams and think of how big your Big Ü can get, and then pull yourself up with your own shoelaces.

Why 2: Changing times

One hundred years before the first publication of this book, the world was coming out of the First World War. So terrible were the events of that conflict, that another such conflict was unthinkable. We know now it happened too.

One hundred years later, we have developed amazing technologies that give us instant one-to-one and many-to-many communication. The dissemination of a book like this to a worldwide audience is one example. The authors and publisher did not leave their offices in order to make it available to a worldwide audience.

In the same way that our actions today are predicated by past errors and previous successes, the world our descendants will inherit will be affected by our imaginings and actions today. What we think, feel and do will ripple down time. We have a responsibility therefore to be mindful of the impact and legacy each of us leaves behind. While it is convenient to think that others from the 7 or more billion people on the planet carry that responsibility – presidents, politicians, business leaders, rock stars, gardeners or writers – it is devolved to each of us individually.

Successful businesses strive for alignment throughout their organisations but often cannot see the areas of misalignment. Leadership models have traditionally been top down. It is now imperative that everyone in the organisation thinks of leadership coming from within, from the inside out.

The precursor to allowing this to happen is to ensure clarity over an organisation's vision, strategy and goals. It's important to be transparent throughout. Each team member should understand their role, the difference they make and the part that they play in getting a business where it wants to be.

This principle even applies to whole countries and eventually to the way we all live and act on the planet. We tend to see a divide between governments and the populace and forget that politicians are souls trying to discover their Big Ü, too. A large ego, in the classic lowercase sense, is just an indication of how disconnected someone has become from their soul.

Some countries, and large organisations, have made massive profits from raw materials and by maintaining a disparity between the rich and poor. The so-called First, Second and Third Worlds are by-products of the Duality.

It could all be so very different. If we look through a different lens, with 20/20 hindsight and foresight, we can observe how nature survives, grows and expands. We are starting to discover the beauty and magnificence of what it does and how it does it.

We now have an amazing collective repository of knowledge accessible to everyone who has an Internet connection. With 'eyes, ears and noses in the sky', we also have the ability to measure what is going on from a planetary perspective. Supercomputers can model and predict current and future rates of consumption of energy and resources. We can innovate our way out of the current way we impact the planet.

If we see ourselves as souls sharing a ride together with other souls on a spaceship we call Earth, it gives a new perspective. We now have the 'smarts' evolving from being users of planetary resources to becoming planetary caretakers.

Should we ever set up colonies on the moon or Mars, because Earth's resources become scarce, it is imperative that we don't migrate there with the same mindset. Any raw materials on other planetary bodies should stay there. The Earth is plentiful enough to support the whole food chain and unlimited energy is beaming to us from the sun daily.

Why 3: Making a difference

Humankind is poised with a golden opportunity to evolve into a bright future. What's more, each of us can contribute to this shift by taking responsibility for our own evolution.

We are fortunate to possess a deep, rich and wide esoteric repository of spiritual wisdoms from the East. We now have augmented our knowledge with analytical 'Western' thinking, which has given us a deep understanding of the Material World. We have models of how the atomic and subatomic worlds operate and an unprecedented ability to see across space, and back in time, to a theoretical point of when all we see came about.

We have a sense of where we came from and ideas of where we might be heading. We are starting to understand our pivotal role in the overall scheme of things. We are not the end result of an evolutionary process but are just experiencing one blink of the cosmic eye. If we survive another millennia, we know everything will be as radically different as our modern society would appear to someone time travelling from a thousand years ago.

We are already living twice as long as our ancestors from a few centuries ago. While advances in medicine can theoretically extend longevity still further, modern lifestyles are creating an obesity crisis which is limiting lifespans and quality of life. This is the nature of Duality.

Generally though, we can expect to have greatly extended working lives, which opens up opportunities for achieving far more at every stage of our lives. We can now develop our minds, our hearts and our souls further, wider and deeper than our ancestors ever did. If we are going to be working for 20 or even 30 years longer than our parents, it's a good idea to find occupations that are enjoyable. It will be easier to stick at jobs that give us real meaning and a sense of purpose.

There is an increasing level of understanding that our heart centre is an active mind centre in constant and bidirectional communication with our brains. Our hearts like to be loved and like to give love. A heart bathed in love also helps us to live more healthily for longer.

What's even more significant is that when two, or more, hearts are in love with what they are doing, they achieve a coherence and a connection at an ethereal level. A collection of heart-centred Big Ü's creates a sum which is greater than its parts. The potential of this to scale across whole organisations, countries and the planet is significant.

We can shift from a mindset of competition and survival of the fittest to one where cooperation and evolution of the whole is paramount. While this might sound a little utopian and impractical, it is possible that an alternative stance will lead us to a world that runs out of resources.

We are in a unique position where our self-awareness allows us to get involved with steering the direction of our own evolution. For some, this might take the form of integration of technology with our bodies. Wearable technology already allows us to extend our senses. For example, hearing aids have been around for many years and optical implants are starting to give sight to the visually impaired.

One aspect of living in a Duality, which is not widely recognised, is that our brains, and other mind centres, are not just generators of thought but also receivers of thought forms. When we tap into this innate, yet often nascent facility we are able to use our self-awareness to extend our own senses.

This leads us to a place where we can make a real difference.

Why 4: You have a dream

The two halves of our brains give us an amazing ability to work on the detail and hold the big picture at the same time. It is incumbent upon us to make the 'picture' as big as possible while not skimping on detail. Martin Luther had a dream. JFK committed to landing humans on the moon within a decade because it was hard.

So what dream can your right brain conjure up that can inspire your left brain to work out how to deliver it? Once the dream is defined, it is fun to ask yourself, 'So what will happen next?'

Take this book for example. We hope several readers take the challenge and opportunity to step into their Big Ü. This would make the authors happy indeed. What would make the authors ecstatic is what happens when their Big Ü makes an impact in the world. As you will see, when the collective benefits, everybody benefits.

Our right brain big picture and dream is for humans to become responsible for steering their own evolution to the highest possible states of awareness and enlightenment. Our left brains will deliver some of the mechanisms in words and accompanying resources, such as the meditations that accompany this book.

Our right brains are comfortable that the right brains of others will have bigger and better dreams, while their left brains are more than capable of joining the dots.

It is worth understanding the true nature of dreams as they are a special type of thought form. They percolate up to our conscious mind from the vast repository of our unconscious mind. In turn our unconscious mind is our conduit to the even greater wisdom and knowledge which resides in the Superconsciousness.

The significance here is that all dreams and daydreams, no matter how weird or fanciful, are realisable in some form. Be mindful that some dreams do arrive in a metaphorical form. Furthermore, if you can dream of something, or just imagine it, it is possible for it to crystallise in some form in the Material World.

Our job, and opportunity, is to become the agent that helps that dream to become reality. It is perhaps here that lies the biggest challenge, and opportunity, for a Big Ü. Our small ü will by its nature have a dream and think that someone else should do it. If you have had an idea, and done nothing with it, and seen it come on the market a few years later then you will have experienced this happening.

On the other hand, it is incumbent on our Big Ü to have big dreams and to see them through to completion. This naturally takes energy, effort, patience and resolve.

If we know what seeds our dreams is our unconscious mind and the Superconsciousness, it is also incumbent on our Big Ü to forge a strong connection with them. Again daily meditation is the key here.

We should also be mindful that the manifestation of dreams into reality is the gauntlet thrown down for your ego by your soul. While all of this might seem somewhat ethereal, your Big Ü must keep one foot firmly grounded in the Material World.

Any resistance you encounter in making your dreams into reality is only a sign that there is an easier way or a better timing. At the same time, any time you get a helping hand or boost in fortune, it's a sign you are on the right path. So dream on, dream up and dream big and, as Lennon sang, know that you are not the only dreamer.

How 1: Time and space

It is prudent to give our Big Ü the time and space to develop naturally. We cannot emphasise enough that treating our evolving Ü to at least ten minutes of some me time is paramount.

Meditation, though, is not something we do for just ten minutes with our eyes closed. With a little practice, we can maintain the meditative state, with our eyes open throughout the day. This stillness gives space.

Whether you meet someone face to face or virtually, be mindful of the space between you. Give time for the dialogue to flow naturally.

When you enter a room, be mindful of how moods can be sensed in the air. This same space can be utilised by a Big Ü. If you sense a tense atmosphere, enter the eyes open meditative state and beam unconditional love into the room, and into the hearts of anyone in there. You will soon sense the room soften.

The intent of the authors lies in the space between these words. A composer instils their emotions into the space between notes.

When we breathe, we should be mindful of the space between the in and the out breath, and the out and the in breath.

This is the special space in time when the conscious and unconscious minds are the closest. It's in this space where dreams can percolate into our awareness.

When you are working creatively, enter the eyes open meditative state and slow down the breath. This has the effect of creating more space in time. You will find that tasks fit into the time available and you get more done in less time.

This is one of the most secret, yet most subtly powerful, time management techniques. By focusing our attention on the present, the perfect future is presented to us, just in time and without us wasting time fretting over its arrival or method of delivery.

How 2: Success and fulfilment

Success and fulfilment are often seen as being mutually exclusive. It is thought that you can't have your cake and eat it after all.

In business, the return on shareholder value is seen as a measure of success. Sometimes realising it comes at a cost, where those at the top of the tree can become stressed and time poor. Something has to give.

Disillusionment, burnout and even ill health can follow. This leads to the questioning of the why, the what and wherefore of it all.

Conversely, some people seek fulfilment where they make a difference in the world and where the happiness of others comes first. Such philanthropy can come at a price, too, in the form of lack of financial success.

So success and fulfilment are two dualistic ideals that we may have had to choose between in the past. What if instead of choosing between having either one or the other, you could have both at the same time?

From a shamanic and spiritual perspective, they are represented by male and female energies. When we know this, the secret to having both at the same time is revealed.

Along with the male energy of success comes fear. We might hold the fear of the share price dropping. Love is the antidote to fear, and a female energy.

So if we have fallen out of love with success and the price we have to pay for it, all we have to do is think of what would have to change so we could fall in love with it again.

If we are fulfilled in our endeavours but feel we are not being rewarded for them, bring some male energy to the party. Ask yourself what practical concrete changes would have to be made to increase your return on investment of love.

How 3: Seek and discover

There are two ways to look for something. We can look inside ourselves and use our mind to seek out what is true. We can also look outside, into the real world, and see what we find.

Seek and you will find, it is said, but also if you just keep looking all the time, there is no space to actually discover anything. If you want to really discover what you are here for, you only have to seek out the patterns in your life and your true path will be revealed.

When we end up on our true path, there is much joy in seeing how events unfold without effort. You can think of this path as being a golden thread on which our whole life unfolds. Everything we do today is attached by this thread to everything that has gone before. Likewise our future lies on this same thread.

Imagine then if there is a future version of you who knows what you have to do right now in order to step into your Big Ü. All you have to do is to give your golden thread a pull, to let your perfect future Ü know that you are seeking and wanting to discover. Then ask for a sign.

This is a good thing to do just before you go to sleep. Ask for a dream which will help. Ask for an event or coincidence to unfold the following day. Then forget you have asked and take joy in the unexpected way the unexpected arrives unexpectedly.

You weren't expecting three uses of the word unexpected in that last sentence, were you? Well we certainly weren't when we unexpectedly wrote it.

This is a self-serving example of how our Big Ü can receive wisdom and insights merely by setting up the conditions for them to arrive.

How 4: Focus and stillness

There are so many demands on our time and attention these days from email, social media and the people who rely on us. As a result, our never ending to-do lists often don't get done.

One of the biggest issues today in the workplace is lack of focus. Some people keep checking their phones, even when they are not vibrating or flashing at them. Some may be worried they might be missing out and others use it as pretence of busyness or importance.

People worry about making decisions without input from all stakeholders, so meetings become elongated and beget other meetings. The world has gone 24x7 and nobody stands still for fear of missing out.

Let us share a simple, and unusual, trick you can use to shorten meeting times and to reach consensus more quickly. At the start of a meeting, get everyone to switch their devices off, or into flight mode. Then get everyone to breathe in sync for seven in and out breaths, and then start the meeting.

This is all you have to do in order to bring everybody's focus into the room and to redirect it from where it was heading before, and after, the meeting. As you have done something a little weird, you will have interrupted their thought flow and brought their attention to bear on the meeting at hand.

In the next meeting, extend the breathing time still further and then you can introduce some other techniques. When it comes to making any decision in the meeting, rather than asking people what their head thinks, ask them what their heart feels. Ask if they are in love with the idea and if not, ask what would have to change for them to fall in love with it.

By changing minds, you change direction, and all that is required is a little stillness.

Energy 1: The power of the breath

Our breath does more than keep us alive. It is the provider of our creative spark, too. Our inspirations arrive on the in breath and our aspirations are delivered on the out breath. These are the two halves of the respiration process. As our neurons do not store any oxygen, it must be delivered through our bloodstream.

Our breath does more than bring in oxygen and dispose of carbon dioxide; it is the prime generator of chi, or life force. That is why it is used so much in meditation and yoga. It also primes the pump of our creative spark and literally inspires us. It is obvious then that shallow breathing will deliver less inspiration than deep breathing, where the diaphragm is engaged.

As we breathe in, we are breathing in new life. When we breathe out stale air, we are releasing our old life, along with old feelings, emotions and thoughts. The breath is not just essential for life but it is also cathartic and cleansing.

As our thoughts are singular in their nature, tuning into the breath also happens to be one of the best ways of calming and controlling the wanderings of our inner chatter.

If something diverts our attention during the day, we can get back to our centre by moving our focus to the breath. If someone makes your blood boil, take three deep in and out breaths before reacting. You and they will be thankful for the space and clarity this brings.

In meetings, become mindful of how you and others are breathing. Breathe deeply and in a rhythmic manner and you will calm the energies in the room and bring everyone to focus and cohesion. A Big Ü does this from a place of quiet power, not for reasons of control.

Energy 2: Synchronisation

One of the roles of a Big Ü is to synchronise and embrace paradoxes in the Duality. The ability to simultaneously hold both views is the essential skill here. Logic and reason must support emotions and feelings.

A Big Ü has both an eye for detail and for the grander vision. It sees how activity in the present is predicated by experiences in the past and how it will form the perfect future. They are perfectly balanced and poised in space and time.

In one model of the world, we operate with the free will to change everything and anything. Another model holds that everything is pre-ordained. To a Big Ü, this paradox is as comfortable to sit with as the notion that atoms are both particles and waves. It is useful to be able to use either model in different circumstances.

To help with synchronisation, there is a simple breathing technique we can use to fire up and energise our left and right brains. It comes from the yogic tradition and there are many variants of it. The simplest version just requires us to hold one nostril closed with our index finger while we breathe in and out through our other nostril.

After doing this four or five times through one nostril, repeat it through the other nostril. It is somewhat esoteric, rather than physiological, but breathing through our left nostril energises our right brain and right nostril breathing activates the left brain.

We can then extend this hemispheric synchronisation by ensuring our head, heart and gut are brought into alignment, especially when making decisions.

Further synchronisation in a temporal context can then be applied with a simple test. When moving forward, consider whether your actions will propel you further down your golden thread or carry you away from it. Opportunity is confirmation of the former and adversity the latter.

Energy 3: Power centres

As we are made of particles of matter, like the atoms we are made from, we are also waves of potential.

These waves of energies are amplified where there are conglomerations of neurons. So we have active centres capable of sending and receiving such waves all over the body. The main points of activity are known as chakra centres in the spiritual traditions of the East.

Our chakras are energised by the breath and can be stimulated through meditation and healing modalities such as acupuncture, massage and reiki.

At a physiological level, chakras are affected by the health of the organs and tissues in close proximity to them. At a psychological level, chakras can be influenced by our internal moods and external events.

For example, if we spend time in a toxic, non-loving environment, our heart chakra will be weakened. If we are not allowed to speak our truth, our throat chakra becomes compromised.

People who have blocked energy centres tend to close in upon themselves and hide their talents. They may have been hurt in the past and made a fool of themselves, so tend to keep a low profile. If you spot them taking time off with illness, it is a sure sign they are compromised in some manner.

Conversely, get all your staff loving what they do and your customers and suppliers will love working with them. The orders will then find you. Give them job security, you will strengthen their sacral chakra. Share your vision and you will charge up their third eye.

Even if you think of these centres as being esoteric or metaphorical, you can use these notions intuitively. You can change and supercharge your language to good effect here. Rather than saying you merely like something, try telling a co-worker, or family member, how much you love what they do and how they go about it. You will see them positively beaming.

Energy 4: Entering the flow state

A Big Ü using its fully alive powers operates in the flow state. This is a place where radical breakthroughs just happen.

Here there is no need to gather yet more information or more answers to more questions. Permission or acceptance is no longer required as you simply operate from your truth.

We should be mindful at all times of the thought patterns that prevent us from entering this special state. If you are harbouring self-doubt or feelings of worthlessness, and lack of self-love, this blocks the flow.

Something weird happens to time when we are in this flow state; we seem to always have enough of it. We get what needs to be done just in time and what we need to help us on our way also seems to show up, just in time.

Our left and right brains and gut and heart minds all experience time in slightly different ways. Our left brain sits inside time and our right brain outside time. Bizarrely, our gut and heart minds operate slightly ahead of time and 'know' things just before we become consciously aware of them.

When our inner chatter reduces to zero, the passage of time alters. We enter the zone where tasks seem to get done in the time frames we have set for them.

With a quiet mind, we become better able to spot coincidences and pick up thought forms that can help and inform us. This is the state where light-bulb moments arrive.

It is the place that Archimedes was in when he exclaimed, 'Eureka. I have found it.' Incidentally and apocryphally, Archimedes was in the bath when this happened. Water is the conductor of what mystics refer to as the 'universal mind stuff'. This is why we sometimes have ideas in the shower, or when walking near water.

THE BIG Ü

KEY TAKEAWAYS

Our mind is both conscious and unconscious.
For every thought, a not-thought exists.
Duality can be harmonised into a new reality.
The two hemispheres of our brain have two different experiences.

COMPANION MEDITATION: WHOLE MIND HARMONISATION

The first part of this meditation is best done with eyes open and it shows you how to get in the zone, or flow state, where your two brain hemispheres synchronise. The second half opens up a permanent connection between your head, heart and gut minds to help you always make the right decision.

QUESTIONS TO PONDER

How full is your glass exactly?
When were you last truly happy and at peace?
Why have you not fulfilled your true potential?
What would make all your hard work worth it?

Part Three
Superconsciousness

'When your mind is fully in enmeshed in Superconsciousness it becomes centred in bliss. You are then at the level of the soul.'

Paramahansa Yogananda

Superconsciousness

IN THE SUPERCONSCIOUS state, we become fully conscious of our own consciousness. We become able to be both self-aware and super-aware. We are immersed in an awareness of the bigger picture and gain the ability to tap into an unlimited source of wisdom.

Here there is no conflict with the notion of Duality as we are both the particle and the wave – both the ocean and the raindrop. We realise that we can change the size and power of the wave on the surface of that ocean by altering the particles in the depths of water below.

There are recognised pathways to reach a state of Superconsciousness. Top athletes use visualisation techniques to get into this special zone. A trainer might tell a runner to visualise the clock with a second shaved off their time, picturing themselves winning the race before they have actually run it. This simple technique makes what is seemingly impossible both possible and doable. To achieve that result, the athletes are totally present and mindful of the moment, creating their own reality.

When we tap into Superconsciousness, we are operating at the quantum level. Fortunately we are all equipped with a very sophisticated quantum computer, in the form of our brain and our whole nervous system. In the quantum world, all possibilities coexist. By adjusting our consciousness, we can influence the quantum layers. By using the power of intent, and by tuning in to whatever it is we want to create, it will arrive in a tangible form.

We are not so much bringing atoms or sub-atomic particles into existence here but real world outcomes. This could be anything from a revolutionary new business product, which will take your company to new heights, or a change in your relationship with your partner.

It is prudent to detach ourselves from the actual mechanisms here and focus on the why and not the how. One reason for this is that the fear that something may not manifest is equally as powerful in the quantum world as the desire for that outcome. Our visions should therefore be set and temporarily forgotten about.

Moving consciousness

The real key to tapping into the Superconsciousness lies in learning how to move awareness to different parts of our bodies. When we become aware of our big toe, this transfers our consciousness there.

A nagging toothache will be dragging our attention away from what we are working on towards the source of distress, and the future prospect of a trip to the dentist.

Step one in accessing the Superconsciousness requires us to become an observer of our thoughts by moving our awareness to the pineal gland at the centre of our brain, at the top of our brainstem.

This is the gateway for external thought forms to arrive and a place where we can observe the ruminations of our conscious mind, from a detached perspective. The companion meditation will allow you to experience this.

After a while, we can learn how to operate with our eyes open from this place. It is as if we are looking at the back of our eyeballs, an observer looking at the observer.

The next stage is the key to all successful manifestation and that is to allow our hopes and dreams to come from our heart centre. We can take the fear that something might not happen from our lower mind in the gut and bring it to our heart.

At the same time, bring the desire for something to occur from the head down to the heart. Then send out your intention solely for what would happen when what you desire manifests, and leave the rest to the universal mind.

Entanglement and de-tanglement

So the Superconsciousness sits outside space and time and underpins Duality and the Material World. You can think of the world around us as crystallising out from this collective mind. Our minds then cause ripples and distortions in its fabric that can then come into being.

The Superconsciousness contains all thought forms of all living beings, past, present and future. This includes the sentience of all things in nature including not just dogs, ants and trees but mountains, oceans, whole planets, moons and stars.

The Superconsciousness is not a massive Wikipedia based on words and language. A dog knows how to give and receive unconditional love. Ants know how to work collectively and for the common good. Trees communicate with each other silently. Mother Earth holds the wisdom of how to create a biosphere. The sun knows how to create and maintain planets in stable orbits. If sentient life exists elsewhere in the universe, it will be adding to the collective pool of wisdom too.

We can choose what aspect of the Superconsciousness we want to tap into. By way of example from the natural world, artificial intelligence researchers can study an ant colony, and work out ways to get nanobots to emulate its behaviours.

The aspect of the Superconsciousness, though, that we most strongly resonate with is us. Our past memories are stored there and we can tap into them, to varying degrees. Our future memories also reside there.

So if something in the past or future concerns us, our monkey mind can circle incessantly on the what ifs and maybes.

Apart from consuming our attention and affecting our efficiency, we also strengthen them and feed and fuel our concerns.

Learning how to detach from events and thoughts and feelings of the past allows us to move on. At the same time, envisioning and imagining a new world for our Big Ü to inhabit has the effect of entangling us with our perfect future. So we stop being pulled back by the past and get pulled along to where we want to be.

As well as our own past and future thoughts, we start to pick up thought forms from co-creators and from people we love. This flow is bidirectional. If someone comes to your mind, they might be thinking of you and the phone may even be about to ring.

A new freedom

A Big Ü so entangled ends up achieving what at first seems miraculous. It bathes in good fortune and produces work of high calibre. Stress lines fall away and people might ask if they have had treatment.

There is no need to switch off from the fearful, sad or bad stories in the press. A Big Ü is fully empathetic and sympathetic and sometimes able to offer a different context or alternative perspective.

At the same time, a Big Ü is making its own news and doesn't have to shout about it, as it is in quiet power. If you could see the surface of the ocean of Superconsciousness, you would notice that the waves a Big Ü is creating are not only large but sinusoidal.

A noisy mind generates smaller choppy waves, whereas a coherence of thought forms creates smooth waves that are directed towards a shore upon where they are best to land.

Like all the concepts in this book, it is not so important that the idea of Superconsciousness is true. Merely by imagining that it exists, we can make ripples in the pond. In fact, if you doubt its existence, your doubtful thought forms will limit your ability to tap into it.

This is similar to worrying about whether you

are meditating correctly. If you are worried about getting it wrong, then that worry is limiting its effectiveness.

When you do tap into the Superconsciousness regularly, there is no need to do it consciously as it just happens and becomes second nature. If we acknowledge its existence, and notice we are being agnostic here, it seems to like to be thanked and recognised.

See your brain as a communication device that is able to access the Superconsciousness and your Big Ü will discover a new sense of freedom. No longer do you have to worry about coming up with new ideas, as if they come from inside you.

Just let them in, as and when they arrive.

Why 1: Fire in your belly

We are life itself, as a self-aware embodiment of the universe. We have life running through our veins, minds, heart and body. When we feel the fire in our belly, we feel fully alive and passionate while also maintaining complete calmness and peace.

We sit calmly in the place where life is magical, miracles are the norm and abundance flows. We know we are a child of the earth and sun and a conduit for all wisdom.

If ever life feels hard and becomes a struggle however, we know there is a misalignment, and possibly a disconnection, to be found. Our belly is the first place to look for any such disquiet and our gut can be consulted with.

You can ask it if you have taken a wrong turn or if there is an easier way. Have you perhaps aligned yourself with the wrong partners or embarked on the wrong project at a non-ideal time? Have you been less than clear with your boundaries and expectations?

As our gut is a wise but primitive mind, it will respond with a yes or a no. What then happens is that a ripple is sent out across the Superconsciousness that an answer is required. It comes back, often within seconds, in the form of a feeling or a knowing. Our heart centre and third eye are the gateways for these responses.

When you realign yourself with the correct guidance, your belly ignites again. You know you are back on path and on to a good thing. What happens next is more magical than you can ever imagine. As your gut, heart and head have engaged themselves in unison, a sign arrives. It can be in the form of an email you are not expecting from a long lost or new contact, or even in a sales order or tax refund that comes out of the blue.

This has the effect of providing unlimited fuel for what fires us up and never goes out. You can spot somebody so driven by their demeanour. They seem to have limitless energy for themselves and others. While they are driven to get their stuff done, they seem to have virtually unlimited capacity to help others.

As they are tapped into the source of all wisdom, the solutions that they come up with seem wise beyond years and elegant in their simplicity. The ways they help others become scalable. So one simple action ends up helping many people. At the same time, their own outputs are customisable and re-deployable.

The fire in our belly enables us to be a kind of superhero. It fires up an inner knowing that we can actually do anything we set our minds to, while living a big life doing big things.

This of course kindles fires in the bellies of others. Like all the techniques in this book, people around you will want a bit of it. You will know who is ready to be lit up and who might get over excited by being imbued with superpowers.

If this sounds like a responsibility has suddenly landed on your shoulders that you didn't want to carry, fret not. When transferring the flame, imagine it rises up from your belly into your heart centre. Pass it silently from your heart, with unconditional love, to the heart of the recipient. Their heart then, not their head, will know what to do with it and when to accept the transfer.

If this sounds a bit like magic, it kind of is. The fire in our belly enables our supreme performance to flourish, transform and magnify.

Why 2: Supreme performance

The very thought of being able to perform at our peak all of the time might fill you with excitement or dread. If it excites you, that's great and you should seize the day and go for it with abandon. The Superconsciousness is a free resource. If you have invested in this book and listened to the companion meditations, you have all the tools that you need at your disposal.

The thought of performing at your best, however, can also seem daunting. What if you burn out? How can you possibly keep to a new level of consistency and maintain it? Why you? Why not leave it to someone else to step up to the plate?

The source of such thinking lies in the Superconsciousness itself. If these doubts percolate to the surface, just meditate on where they have come from in the first place. You may then think about times when you thought you were performing supremely only for the wheels to come off the bus. These types of memory are real and should not be dismissed. They are merely there as guardians and guides.

Fortunately the Superconsciousness also holds the answer. Meditate on what you would have to do differently next time so that you didn't end up blowing a fuse, or losing your rag.

A more subtle shift in thinking allows the Big Ü to transcend any notions of failure. As Yoda said, 'Do or do not, there is no try.'

If you see yourself as a conduit for the Superconsciousness, it gives us a new reason why we should aim for supreme performance. All the answers to all we seek lie there, including solutions on how to tackle any problem or opportunity, despite how insurmountable they may seem at first.

The main reason why a Big Ü operates superconsciously is because it is easier and so much less stressful. Once you are aware of its existence, the more you ignore it, the more it will knock on the door. It's as if it is daring you to step up when, in fact, it's just the best version of you in the future asking for your assistance.

When we get over any initial resistance, it immediately gets so much easier. The benefits that come along are far-reaching. Not only do you discover an easier way to be but other people find it easier to have you around. You get invited in to play at levels and in ways you previously thought were inaccessible to you.

What you had imagined would be hard work, if you were called to perform at that level, starts to become a breeze. What was foreign and unimaginable becomes second nature. Soon you find that you have a new job title or role in life.

This new role is not something you have to create or invent. You will find people will tell you what you do that is so valuable to them. You end up not only ditching old, unworthy thought patterns but the old tasks you used to perform that kept you so busy.

You see the old ways in context for what they truly were. Some of them gave you essential learnings and experience. Others kept you being a 'busy fool,' being creatively uncreative at stepping into your brilliance.

When you eventually do step up, any notions of guilt vaporise quickly as you are so busy performing supremely at whatever your Big Ü was called to do. The biggest why comes to meet you when you finally realise everything has become so much easier.

Why 3: Explosive creativity

Where performance is perhaps a quantitive measure of our output, creativity is a measure of quality of output. It is also a measure of how well we are allowing the Superconsciousness to flow through us.

Creativity is contagious. Collective creativity, when Big Ü's co-create, leads to a culture of creativism. A company operating in this manner is a force to be reckoned with and will always be one step ahead of its competitors. When competitors do eventually catch you up, you will have already moved on.

It is not sufficient to be creative for the mere sake of being creative. Business can become great at introducing new services and products but there has to be a reason why. Creativity achieves the best results when it has a direction.

This does not mean randomness does not have a role in the creative process. In chaos theory, it is postulated that the beating of a butterfly's wings can be the trigger for a hurricane or typhoon on the other side of the planet. The creative spark from a Big Ü can have the same effect. Sometimes it is not the seed idea but the spin-off that creates the biggest waves.

A Big Ü acts as a catalyst for change, where change itself is the only driver. When we go 'meta', it drives a change that makes a real difference. In Greek, the word meta means 'beyond' or 'above'. So when a creative idea comes your way, before jumping into it with both feet, meditate on where it might lead. If and when the idea is realised, muse on what might happen as a result. Then consider on what might happen when that secondary result is realised, and so on. Perform this iteration as many times as you can and you will discover a new reason why.

This sets up the conditions for your creativity to explode. The Big Ü knows that it can now forget about the end why and just concentrate on the first creative seed. This book and companion meditations is a perfect example. When this seed germinates, it becomes the first domino that knocks a whole chain down effortlessly.

Any seed requires nurturing and tending. It has to be planted in the right soil and receive just the right amount of water and sunlight. Too much of either can hamper its growth. Sometimes they are best left to their own devices and not watched continuously. In each seed of course is embedded the ability to grow more seeds.

Explosive creativity actually requires that we are sometimes mindfully lazy and that we take our foot off the gas from time to time. You will find others are germinating similar seeds but with different outcomes in mind.

Observing best practice allows the cross-fertilisation of ideas and makes our seeds stronger and more resilient.

We should also be mindful that creativity is not limited to the traditional creative arts, or marketing. We can be creative about our accounts, how we dress, how we run meetings and how we interact with people in general. Where it helps greatly is in tackling tasks you think of as chores or being boring.

Apart from the creative output itself, it is worth bearing in mind that a daily dose of creativity brings in the most amazing benefit.

To be a Big Ü, and to really show up in the world, it is vital that you look after your wellbeing and remain healthy. Daily exercise and watching what you eat helps here of course. When we tap into the Superconsciousness, we channel in the same chi, or life force, used by energy healers. We make ourselves healthier.

Why 4: Harmony and grace

With our performance at its optimum and with our creative juices flowing, we are naturally going to generate excitement, both inside and around us. Inevitably you will start many plates spinning and you, or your loved ones, might worry you might burn out.

To avoid any such overload, it is worth understanding a subtle aspect of the Superconsciousness. It is gentle, kind and supportive by its nature. It is underpinned by unconditional love for all beings. It also likes to receive unconditional love back but this is not a condition of connecting with it. That is the very nature of unconditionality. The universe is fundamentally benevolent, otherwise we wouldn't even be here to observe it.

In time, the connection to the Superconsciousness becomes something you don't switch on when you need a creative boost. The connection is both permanent and pervasive. Its presence will be felt in every email you send and every time you speak to someone. It is there while you are dreaming.

More significantly you will be in constant contact with your soul and slowly and steadily become its embodied agent in the Material World. Eventually, you release all tensions and worries and truly go with the flow. You then enter a zone where you exude harmony and grace.

This gives us a deep feeling of peace, beauty and presence which spreads around us. We can see others and be seen in the full glory of who we are. When we are seen and acknowledged in this manner, it is truly a blessing. This fulfils a fundamental need for any human being, that of being loved and being able to give love.

The conventional interpretation of the term ego is replaced by a soul–ego connection and our essence becomes open for all to experience. We do not force ourselves on others and we don't think for a moment that we have all the answers. We don't think we are any better than anyone else or promote ourselves above others. We are humble and walk in grace. This allows us to harmonise what is disharmonious.

A martial artist gets fully centred and focused from their core so that they can defend themselves, whichever angle they are attacked from. A Big Ü operates from the same kind of stance, yet without having to harbour any thoughts of attack, fear or threat.

The electromagnetic field generated by our heart centre is hundreds of times stronger than the field generated by our brains, and can be detected metres away.

When two people fall in love, their heart fields

have entangled. This entanglement stretches across space and time to eternity.

When a group of people come together with a common vision, operating to common and lofty values, the fields from their heart centres harmonise. When two sine waves are in synchronisation, and harmony, they fuse together and this field gets stronger. Get a whole company operating with hearts in harmony and you will truly have a force to be reckoned with.

Again, all such power should be used wisely and sagely. Imagine customers and suppliers getting their hearts in sync with yours. They will simply love to work with you and even take their joy back home with them to their family and loved ones.

So adopting a position of harmony and grace is not a weak, supine position where people can walk over you. It is a position of immense strength. If for a moment it is used for your own betterment to the detriment of others, this brings in an immediate fall from grace. When it is used for your own betterment only, it is strengthened. When it is used for the betterment of others it is amplified.

How 1: Let your soul lead

Throughout your life, you will have been in communication with your soul. While reading this book, our hope is that you've thought a little more about it, and maybe sensed it.

Its existence cannot be measured or proven, only intuited. It works silently and without any need for us to acknowledge it. When we strengthen the connection to our soul, our Big Ü just ends up getting bigger again.

There is a simple exercise we can all do to make its presence known and felt. Think of something that you would like more of in your life. Rather than money or a new car, choose something intangible like happiness, peace or love.

Then think about a real world situation that involves an interaction with others that you are facing which could benefit from bringing this to bear. Think about how it would it help exactly and what would then happen as a result. Next you do something a little out of the ordinary, you do nothing.

Just imagine if the onus did not lie with you at all to improve the situation. Ask your soul for its help and guidance. Ask it, too, if it could sort things out at a soul-to-soul level with the person, or situation, you would love to help.

Now let go of the mechanism for the resolution and just become an observer of the outcome.

This strategy takes a little trust but of course costs nothing to try and requires virtually no investment of time or energy on your part. Herein lies its genius, which becomes your genius.

To benefit from this approach only requires us to be comfortable with the notion that the Superconsciousness exists and that we might all have a soul. When the resolution arrives, and it will, it doesn't prove either exists. It merely proves thinking that they might is all that is required.

How 2: Get in alignment

To maximise our connection with the Superconsciousness, it is vital we are in alignment.

Strangely enough this is helped by a straight spine as this aids the flow of subtle energies. The alignment we are really seeking is one where our spirit, mind, heart, soul and body are working together, in harmony of course. In physicality, our heart is at the centre of operations.

If our body is depleted through thirst, hunger or lack of any of the necessary nutrients, it will start to complain. Look after it well as it is the vehicle that self-propels you around the Material World.

If we allow thought forms seeded by negative emotions to circulate unchecked around our mind, they will end up afflicting our body in some way or another. This might lead to the depletion of an organ, a joint or a muscle by subtly blocking one of our energy gateways. When the latter happens, we restrict the influence our soul can bring to bear.

Our body, mind and spirit form a triad of health. Ideally we want this to be a balanced equilateral triangle. If one side of this triangle is shortened, it puts stress on the other two. If two sides are afflicted, the triangle distorts and we end up being misaligned.

If this occurs, we can actually tap into the Superconsciousness for guidance and to help to steer us back on path. We can ask whether we can deal with the situation ourselves or whether we should go to a doctor or therapist.

If we are to fix it ourselves, we only have to look at our lifestyle and meditate on the thought forms that are circulating around our mind.

If external help is needed, ask for a sign, or ask a friend who has had the same type of problem and go and see someone who can help with your realignment.

How 3: Source-ery

The word 'source' comes from the Old French 'sourse' which means 'a rising, a beginning, the fountainhead of a river or stream'.

When working in, around and with Superconsciousness, we should always be aware that we are conduits and that the Superconsciousness flows through us, not from us. To reiterate, this flow is self-serving as when this happens, a sorceress or sorcerer becomes superconscious.

Tapping into this stream of all wisdom involves us moving to a place beyond logic, reason and belief. Here we don't think about the how, when or where. It involves just 'be-ing' in a place of 'know-ing' and 'allow-ing'. We are rewarded, in this special place, with unconditional love, kindness and compassion.

All sorceresses and sorcerers use different tools, talismans and methodologies to access this place. Meditation is the most common tool, bearing in mind that there are many methods of accessing the meditative state. In times gone by, ritual, hallucinogens, dancing and chanting would be used to enter the trance state. These days, we can use an app on our smartphones, which is somewhat safer and more reliable and repeatable.

Some use crystals, cards, runes, numbers,

colours, symbols and sounds to bring their magic into being. When your Big Ü becomes more adept in what are called the 'magical arts', the need for any such props dwindles as you integrate the wisdom in your psyche. Indeed, the most talented adepts go about their work without their presence, and methodologies, being noticeable or detected.

They are able to influence the Material World with just a touch or a thought. Subtlety is the name of the game.

In this space the unknown and unseen become seen and known: it is only magic and sorcery until we know how the trick is carried out.

How 4: Pure and simple

It is tempting and possible to make all this bigness complex. This is a human thing to do. Big impacts are often delivered with a fanfare and lots of razzmatazz.

There is no need to over-dramatise. When a Big Ü is in full flow, three things happen that help to keep things pure and simple.

First, the Big Ü is calm and serene and expends minimal effort in delivering the most amazing results. A single well-timed word, or just a smile or a wink, might be all that is needed. It only has to provide the spark for one soul to connect with another. It's just natural, pure and simple. It does, however, require us to be totally present, and the space in-between merges and becomes one. Its impact, however, can be beautifully magnificent.

Second, a Big Ü is a master of timing. The when is as important as the what and the how.

Third, the recipients of bigness don't necessarily have to appreciate what just breezed into their world. The impact of the change brought to them might not be apparent for many days, months or even years later. They will sense that they have been deeply touched and feel something is now different from before.

When the full impact dawns on someone who

has experienced a Big Ü coming into their world, they will remember back to the exact place and time when it occurred. Now you could contact that Big Ü and thank them. An alternative course of action is simple and that's to just copy what you experienced and pass the treat on to someone else.

A Big Ü operating in this manner is the embodiment of unconditional love and flows and moves through the world with a purity and simplicity which is sublime in its influence.

Energy 1: Unconditionality

When we bestow a random act of kindness upon someone, they are best dispensed with a few caveats in mind.

First, they should be random and not premeditated. We can be guided by our soul on this.

Second, we shouldn't give them out expecting to get one coming back the other way.

Third, and most importantly, we should not expect the recipient to be the person who bounces our kindness back to us. When one does come back our way, we should always express our gratitude.

This is the essence of unconditionality. We do it because we are guided to do so for no reward, other than knowing we touched someone's soul. This generates a sense of appreciation which puts a smile on the face of the recipient. Follow these simple rules of unconditionality and you will be rewarded with infinite possibilities. You will soon discover how what goes around, comes around.

If you would like to take things up a gear, there is a Buddhist practice whereby you first practise loving yourself, then a benefactor, then a friend, then someone neutral and finally an enemy. To love someone with whom you have an unresolved conflict provides a door to step through that takes us from a place of conditional love to one of unconditional love.

By consciously moving to such unconditionality, we synchronise with the underlying sentiment of the Superconsciousness. This moves us to a new level of coherence.

Our Big Ü has no attachments, no expectations and no desires in this place. Here we can be totally present, loving and accepting of everything as it is.

When there is the presence of the Big Ü, all that is illusory and conditional falls away, and what is left is real, vital, pure and simple and passionately alive. This is life, just as it is, free and unconditional.

Energy 2: Prescience

The word prescience can be better understood when it is hyphenated to pre-science. The Superconsciousness operates outside time and space. So all knowledge, past, present and future, from all living beings in all parts of the cosmos is stored in the collective.

Our planet Earth also has a local field of storage known as the noosphere and we are more predisposed to pick up on 'local' information. All moons, planets and stars have similar local fields of collective consciousness too.

So when Da Vinci drew a helicopter, and a parachute should it be required, he was merely tapping into information from the future. We resonate most strongly with energies from our own future self, as well as our own past memories. This means that if we want to know something, we only have to ask ourselves. It is possible and maybe probable that light-bulb moments are nothing more, or less, than 'future memories' leaking back to us in time.

If you are faced with a quandary, ask yourself in the future for an answer, ideally when you are meditating. Then keep a quiet mind and allow the answer to come. You can also write a question on a note and pop it under your pillow at night and you will get an answer, sometimes codified in metaphor, in your dreams.

If you want some direction, ask for a sign and again it will be given but perhaps in a very unexpected form. If the information you need to act on is very important, the message may come in a form that is more insistent and persistent. You can be blocked from one course of action because a more optimal route is available for you. You can also find yourself procrastinating and becoming a busy fool.

In these cases, let frustration abate and be replaced by inspiration. Make haste slowly and wisely.

Energy 3: Opening to channel

Channelling is often associated with mediums connecting with the dear departed, like aunty Ethel or uncle Fred. These days, though, some film stars talk about channelling the person they are playing on screen. Some pop stars say they are 'channelling' an artist from the past, living or dead.

In the context of connecting and working with Superconsciousness, channelling has a different context. It refers to the conscious aspect of our psyche stepping aside so our creative muse can operate through us. The reason why mediums are so-called is that they re-broadcast 'the media of the Superconsciousness'.

It should be noted that information flows from Superconsciousness into Duality and then into the Material World. As transfer is so instantaneous, we are not and should not be conscious of the intermediate steps. The actual mechanism is somewhat academic.

What we actually channel is a moveable feast. Most of the words in this book are channelled, as is the nature of the whole Big Ü project. Mozart channelled his symphonies and Da Vinci his wondrous sketches of flying machines of the future.

We are not restricted to channelling art or

science; we can also channel information from any living animal or plant.

You can also commune with the mountain, the sea, the moon, planets and stars. In order that you don't lose your sense of self, or be influenced by the fairies, our view is that channelling is best done with a practical outcome in mind.

Like all the mechanisms that connect us with Superconsciousness, channelling is nothing new for us. If you have ever been 'in the zone' where creative juices were flowing, you have already acted as a channel.

Daily meditation sets us up well for a channelling session and helps us to remain in the meditative state, with eyes open, throughout the day, while working on creative tasks.

Energy 4: Precognition

Most channelled information comes from outside our physical body and through our brain, with the pineal gland as the gatekeeper. Our lower mind centres, especially the heart and gut, also act as routes for information to come our way.

What is slightly odd about the lower minds is that they act ahead of time. As our gut and heart minds have been active for all our lives, you will have almost certainly already experienced this temporal anomaly but perhaps not recognised its full significance.

If you have ever known who is on the phone just before it rings, you will have tapped into this cognitive centre. If you have ever gone along with something when your heart wasn't in it, then you will have experienced what happens when you ignore or overrule their council.

At the same time our conscious minds are all interconnected in the Superconsciousness, so are all our gut minds. If you go into a room and there is a negative vibe, you can guarantee it is coming predominantly from the lower mind centres of people in that room. Sometimes a person can leave a room and leave a vibe behind.

Hearts detect the states of other hearts. This is also how we fall in love. Remember that, when two hearts intertwine, their fields synchronise.

This of course scales up in business. Start with aligning your head, heart and gut and then get everyone else to follow, and you will create an unstoppable team.

The key to enhancing your precognitive ability is to really understand what the term means. If you are cogniscent of something ahead of time, that information exists somewhere already. This can only be in a place outside space and time. You now know where this is.

Like all the techniques in this book, enhancing our natural precognitive abilities is simple. Just practice and trust.

KEY TAKEAWAYS

Our whole neurology acts as a tuning fork for the Superconsciousness.
Future memories are as accessible as those from the past.
The Superconsciousness underpins Duality and the Material World.
Our heart centre is the conduit for our soul.

COMPANION MEDITATION: ACCESSING SUPERCONSCIOUSNESS

This is an eyes closed meditation that builds a stronger and more open connection with your inner minds, soul and the Superconsciousness. Be sure to keep notes in your journal after listening as you will be tuning into ripples in the pond just by listening.

QUESTIONS TO PONDER

When were you last truly in the zone?
What creation are you most proud of?
How much Me Time do you treat yourself to each week?
What have you done to make the world a better place?

Part Four
Oneness

> *'All differences in this world are of degree, and not of kind, because Oneness is the secret of everything.'*
>
> Swami Vivekananda

Oneness

MOVING TO ONENESS can only be experienced. It is esoteric in its nature. It cannot be understood with logic or with the rational mind.

As such, to embrace Oneness takes somewhat of a leap of faith. We will attempt to describe what it is here and give you some of the keys to discover it. Only your Big Ü can truly appreciate it.

What's more, as it is such an individual experience, it may well be that each of us find it in different manners and to different degrees. A painter might be at one with the scene in front of them and their canvas. A downhill skier can become one with the mountain. An astronaut on a spacewalk can experience Oneness with the cosmos.

Back down on Earth though, where do you even start to find Oneness?

As you will see, the whys are somewhat esoteric and the hows somewhat philosophical. While energies associated with connecting with Oneness are somewhat ethereal, we are fortunate that we have been tapped into them from birth.

Accordingly, the path to finding this elusive place of Oneness requires us to take an imaginary journey backwards and forwards in time.

Unravelling the golden thread

Go back down the timeline of your own golden thread and you will find yourself as a foetus in your mother's womb. Go back to before you were conceived and you will discover you were a mere possibility. Your parents either consciously, or by accident, thought it would be a good idea to bring a small version of ü into the world.

Then continue backwards down the golden threads of your parents and you will discover where their threads started, with the thoughts and doings of your grandparents. Now continue right back down all your ancestors' timelines, back to the time humans evolved, or came from another species, and something will dawn upon you. On planet Earth, there was a time when we were all one. We came from the same seed. Our golden threads all unravel outwards from that same place, which is incidentally another example of singularity. Cosmologists have even extrapolated back to the very dawn of time and think all energy and matter came from one colossal bang. So all stars were once one as well.

Now go forward on your golden thread to a time when you shed your mortal coil. Your atoms will be re-absorbed into the earth, either as ash, vapour or by decomposition. What remains of your soul and wisdom will stay as memories, experiences, feelings and emotions, writings, photographs and perhaps video and audio recordings. These can be consumed and absorbed by others. They are an echo of your marks upon the world. Some of them will be slight, left by your small ü. Hopefully some will linger for longer, dropped into the ocean of Oneness by your Big Ü.

If reincarnation is a model you subscribe to, a future version of you might even 'look yourself up', pick up the end of the thread you left behind and run with it. Timelines intertwine with timelines. Lives beget lives. We simply wouldn't be here if our ancestors had not brought us and our parents and grandparents into the world. Whether we have children or not, our lives will impact in a small, intermediate or big way with others yet to be born.

These ripples are not limited to humankind either. How we treat our pets affects their offspring. The net energy we consume while on the planet affects Mother Earth herself, and all other lifeforms. It is thought that all planets, and stars, are connected to each other right across the cosmos.

As the Native American Indian Chief Seattle said, 'We do not weave the web of life, we are only a strand on it. What befalls the Earth, befalls the sons and daughters of the Earth.'

We can only conjecture what he was referring to as the 'sons and daughters'.

Once something is known, it cannot be unknown. So when our Big Ü becomes aware that every action leads to re-action – the hyphen is intentional – we have to tread mindfully and with purpose.

This is not a warning. It is an opportunity. If you do subscribe to the model of reincarnation, whether it is with the return of a soul or its echo being carried forward in DNA, it makes sense to leave the planet in a better state than when you found it.

As we all come in with no money, there's no point taking it with you. What you can leave behind is your art, your wisdom and your learnings. Together they form a legacy. Add everyone's legacy together in collective Oneness and the sum becomes greater than the parts.

Tuning into Oneness

To envisage this unseen world of Oneness, imagine your golden thread is woven together from four strands. Note that we can even conjecture that these strands are encoded in the four letters that form our DNA. Indeed, our DNA may well be like a tuning fork that allows our consciousness to resonate with the essence of Oneness.

On the first strand lies the guidance we receive from our soul throughout our lifetime. This gives us impetus and momentum to live out our life.

The second strand contains the actions and thoughts expressed by our ego. We can see this as a thought stream that we pass through of everything we are conscious of in our lives.

The third strand is that of unconditional love. We hold this for ourselves, others and for all the conditions that come together to allow us to appreciate the Material World we inhabit.

The fourth strand wraps around these other three and interconnects the Material World, Duality and Superconsciousness into Oneness, making them whole.

When we realise that our lives are actually played out across these strands, we reach a new level of enlightenment.

If we ignore the guidance of our soul on the

first strand, this strand gets weakened and can even snap. If our ego takes control, the second strand can become knotted. The third strand of unconditional love becomes threadbare if not exercised.

All through our lives, though, we are fortunate to be wrapped in the fourth strand.

This holds everything together so we can have the experience of being incarnate on this special planet.

When we understand the interconnectedness of everything, it puts a special onus upon us. What we think, feel and do right now affects the wellbeing of future versions of us, in this life. So it is incumbent upon us to be the Biggest Ü that we possibly can be, if for no other reason than so that we can love our life to the maximum, at least in this incarnation.

If you like the idea of reincarnation, or aim to pass through the pearly gates, or just pass your DNA down the generations, seeing the Oneness in all allows us to go about our lives in a more mindful manner. Every one of our thoughts, feelings and actions drops a pebble in the pond which affects all other life forms and consciousness to some degree or other.

When we really take this on board, it gives us a new motivation and new sense of direction. Each of us is truly capable of being the change.

Why 1: The honour

The very fact that you are reading these words is an honour.

First, we are honoured you have read so far and not put the book back on your shelf.

Second, if you can afford to buy this book and read it, we should be mindful that many people on the planet still can't even read, never mind have the financial wherewithal.

Third, and most importantly, your ability to read this book, and our ability to write it, is only made possible by the ability of the universe to provide the conditions for sentient life to exist. At least two generations of stars have exploded cataclysmically to create the atoms that we are made from. Hundreds of generations of our ancestors have lived and died to imbue our DNA with the essence of us. While you have been alive, many plants and animals have died just to keep you alive.

So being you, and being a Big Ü especially, is an honour.

This means we all carry a level of expectation on our shoulders. Stepping up to become your Big Ü comes first; you should pat yourself on the back for making this move. The next step involves us taking action.

Some may feel that connecting with Oneness

is something to do sitting cross-legged in a cave, chanting 'Om' and staring at their navel. The impact and imprint that a Big Ü makes in the Material World is the real measure of their bigness. This is not something measured in the size of a bank account or even in the size of philanthropic initiatives. It is all about how you experience the world around you.

The Oneness has honoured each of us with the ability to be self-aware in the Material World. This has led to the honour of being able and capable of undertaking this journey to become your Big Ü. It is a kind of self-fulfilling initiative that provides its own momentum.

If we get weighed down by this expectation, we will quickly un-evolve back into being a small ü. So it's a good idea to take baby steps.

Awaken each morning with the notion that the day will bring surprises your way. Sprinkle random acts of kindness out as you go about the day. Be grateful for all the serendipities that fall at your feet. Remember animals and plants need your unconditional love as much as human beings.

So as well as smiling at a stranger, stroke a dog or a cat, hug a tree (literally) and admire a view. Mother Earth appreciates being thanked, too, for the wonder she has created.

If all this sounds a little hippy, go with it.

Trust the process and you will quickly see how rewards come right back at you.

As you change your behaviours, it will be necessary at some point or other for you to take off the mask of your small ü and show the true colours of your Big Ü. This can be scary and a little daunting at first. What you will find, though, is that others start to take their masks off too.

You create a safe environment around you where people no longer feel they have to keep up pretences and erect barriers. They feel safe around you.

The implications inside a business, or any partnership, are immense. The mood changes and even the language changes. Backbiting and gossip is replaced by thoughts of co-creation and mutual success. Confidence grows from small wins, and bigger wins soon follow as you start to bring people to Oneness.

As your Big Ü grows and delivers beyond expectations, and begins to live a life that we love with ease, others will inevitably emulate your behaviour. In the true sense of the word, you become a creator. This is something to honour.

Why 2: The absolute why

We can spend many years of our lives seeking meaning and purpose. Either internally or externally, we strive to articulate who and what we are. We long to know why we are here and what are we here to do.

These deeper questions often arrive when we have a crisis in our lives, lose a loved one or just when we get bored. Disillusionment sets in and we question the point of everything, and ourselves.

Before we go to school, we look to our parents to give us the answers. Children can be heard asking why. At school, we look to our teachers, and some of them do indeed share what they know. When we start work, we hope our bosses know what is going on and tell us what to do and how to do it.

Along the way, we will have read books, seen films and TV, and looked to art, poetry and music for enlightenment. Some will be attracted to religion while others will look towards politicians or celebrities for answers.

All such roads will inevitably lead to some form of disappointment. We make no claims that this book provides the answers either. It is merely designed to point you in the direction of where to look.

Your five senses are designed for you to experience the Material World around you. Most of the time they can be relied on, until you are presented with an optical illusion perhaps. Such devices have been created by scientists to help us actually understand the limitations of our senses.

As quantum physicists have observed, the Material World is not all it seems and is a pervasive illusion. The Duality is less 'real' than the Material World while being a more accurate representation of reality. Half-full glasses are after all half-empty. The first step in awakening our super-senses is the realisation that we can alter probability with our mind alone.

This leads us to discover the Superconsciousness. It is when we tap into it fully that we become even more able to affect the metaphorical rolling of the dice in the Duality. Our dreams then begin to manifest more regularly in the Material World.

These three shifts should provide us with a big enough why in themselves. For a while, we can have a lot of fun and a not inconsiderable amount of success with them. After a while, though, more discontent rears its head when we start to question why yet again.

When we embrace and connect with the Oneness of everything, another why will occur to us at some time or other. This is perhaps the absolute why.

Why would the Oneness separate out to create Superconsciousness, Duality and the Material World in the first place?

Some cosmologists think that what started in a Big Bang, 13 or so billion years ago, might end up in a Big Crunch. Apparently, our 4.5 billion year-old Earth might even be consumed by its own Sun in a further 4.5 billion years or so. When our Sun exhausts its supply of hydrogen, it will swell and become a red giant which will extend outside the orbit of our planet.

These notions can lead to us thinking that everything is ultimately futile and there's no point in even getting out of bed.

What if the Oneness itself did not know why either? What if the whole point of everything is just to allow the experience to unfold to see what happens when this type of four-level universe is created?

If you like the idea of an all-seeing god, then this god may be so minded. After all, eternity is a long time and it might get a bit boring looking down at everything from the clouds.

Imagine, though, if discovering the answer to this absolute why was something a number of Big Ü's were called upon to discover. Now that would be fun.

Why 3: Wholeness

It has been written that the Buddha has said, 'Before enlightenment chop wood and carry water and after enlightenment chop wood and carry water.'

What is different about the chopping and the carrying in both scenarios is our awareness of what we are doing, how we are doing it and why we might be doing it. This is the nature of Duality. Our left brain might pay attention to how finely we chop the wood and assemble it into piles that we can carry easily. Our right brain might be thinking of the feast we will cook on the fire that we make with the same wood later.

The fire that is made with the wood burns and emits heat in the Material World. Thoughts have become manifest. When people assemble around the fire, their consciousnesses will connect together in the collective Superconsciousness. If they are hunter-gatherers, they may be cooking what they ensnared that day. Even though some life was extinguished, that life is giving others life. This is the nature of Oneness.

You can think of the wholeness of everything in two ways – as we are in Duality.

At one time, at the start of time, Oneness got bored and Superconsciousness and Duality distilled from it. One became two at this point.

Incidentally, cosmologists refer to this time as First Light which happened about 400,000 years after the Big Bang. Note that years didn't exist then so the exact time is somewhat irrelevant. What is relevant is that particles and waves were created, as were anti-particles.

When things cooled down a little, the Material World crystallised and densified. Sometime later, we all showed up and started asking why.

Now we are all here, asking questions, we can turn this whole model on its head. As we are made from both particles and waves, we are able to influence outcomes in the Material World by tinkering with the Duality. In turn, the wisdom bank of the Superconsciousness gets bigger and bigger. Finally, Oneness becomes bigger and even more omnipresent and omniscient.

We think of the past creating the future but it could be possible that the future creates what's already past. It's just that we experience the dimension of time as flowing forward.

If all of this sounds overly philosophical, it is. How can this esoteric thinking increase your profits or find you true love?

Well if everything is connected not only in space but also in time, all we have to do to create whatever we desire is to understand the very nature of things. Let your head become the observer and director and start getting used to following your heart. Let you gut guide you, too, and remember your soul is pulling your strings.

Remember at all times that the reality you see is a mirror of what is going on in your mind. Shadows create shadows. Light illuminates dark corners. Should dis-ease or adversity come along, look inside first before going to the doctor or your business coach. When good fortune pops in, see it as confirmation you are on path.

By the way, if you think this is a little repetitious, we are mindfully repeating it as it needs repeating and hammering home. Once you adopt this strategy, getting to wholeness is easy.

Dream your biggest dreams. Tear up your to-do lists and replace them with a to love list. Tackle your to love list by doing the things that you love the most first. Then go out into the world as a walking, talking expression of unconditional love.

Then let your Big Ü out to play and just enjoy what unfolds as a result.

Why 4: The gift

It is a veritable gift to be alive at this time. Recognition of this allows us to comprehend the real beauty of the Big Ü.

Our consciousness is capable of understanding the three aspects of the Material World, the Duality and the Superconsciousness.

Our real gift is to be able to synthesise, harmonise and reintegrate these three parts back into the Oneness from which they came. In Oneness, everything is just as it is.

Here our gift starts to be revealed. We can see and feel how everything connects. It all moves within us and in front of us. The dots are joined and all becomes clear. We see, hear, feel, taste, smell and touch everything as one. At the same time, we know that it is from our individual being that this gift emanates.

Each of our gifts are unique. Our gift has been born from every step we personally have taken, every thought we have had, everything we have felt and all that we have experienced. Our gift is our own meaning, passion and purpose for our life. It is the individual essence of who we are, how we serve and our very presence. This uniqueness is one of the most powerful aspects of a Oneness that decided to separate.

Once we tap into and express this gift, it

enables us to travel down our golden thread with love, ease and grace. We finally find what we have been searching for.

In reality, though, we know that it has found us and become known to us. We now know we have had it all along. It has been within us and part of us every step of the way. We now have the laser focused clarity, the deep knowing, and the feeling of wholeness, peace, bliss, completeness and Oneness. This is truly remarkable, so very perfectly simple and sensually pure.

The gift is us and we are it. We are one. We are totally comfortable being entangled with our golden thread, with all that has gone before us and all that is to eventually become as one again.

There is no pushing, struggling, wanting or seeking. We meditate daily to give ourselves the gift of silence and stillness. Magic then happens as all is gently and miraculously revealed.

We are all incredibly lucky to be who we are. This luck that we are graced and blessed with is nicely infectious. Our very being affects everything around us and whatever we choose to connect with. Just by being your Big Ü enables others to become their Big Ü. This is probably the greatest gift we can give to anyone or anything.

By bestowing this gift on ourselves and others,

meaning is found along with a certain amount of truth. We walk with a surety of step, even while we are not totally sure where we are heading. We are scared and excited in equal measure but feel up for the challenge and the opportunity.

The achievements of others are our achievements, too, but we have no need to lay claim to them. This is a measure of how big we have really become. We also lose the need to shout from the rooftops about how big we have become. Our deeds do the talking and the beneficiaries of our actions spread the word. It is the gift that just keeps giving.

What happens next is quite remarkable. Our golden thread becomes entangled with the golden threads of others. This makes them stronger and allows us to begin to weave rich tapestries where the whole is more beautiful than the sum of the parts.

Our Big Ü just got bigger.

How 1: Purity of consciousness

It is important that we recognise all thought forms are living, moving, active and dynamic. Thoughts don't so much become things, they are tangible things.

The word 'consciousness' drives from the Latin 'con scire' meaning 'to know with', or 'to be privy to'. It originally referred to the insights from within. What we then share with others is a demonstration of our state of consciousness. What they then share with us is a reflection of both their state and our state of awareness.

We can also think of consciousness as having a hierarchical structure, where the starting point is consciousness 'at rest', without any attributes or qualities. Then there is consciousness 'in movement', functioning as the witness. As soon as there is the thought 'I am', it becomes 'embodied' consciousness. Finally, this becomes identified with the body–mind and the 'attached' consciousness.

The process of Oneness involves removing any identification and returning to the witness position. The 'I am' is still present and turning up for duty but observing from a more elevated and detached vantage point. It is only a matter of perspective.

The idea that 'I am' the body, or the mind, is so

entrenched that it is at first hard to detach from. We experience a dream and know it to be unreal on waking. Waking experiences are similarly unreal in other states.

Consciousness nests inside consciousness. Open the first Russian doll and where might you stop?

If all of this sounds a bit deep, bear in mind that in order to experience pure consciousness, we need to let go, lighten up and play. It involves simple, pure surrender and the taking of our awareness and focus to our core and our essence.

Try meditating on these notions for starters and say hello to your inner guru.

How 2: The end of the ego

Our ego has been a wonderful travelling companion. It gives us the sense of who we are and how different we are from every other soul walking around the planet.

It's even been instrumental in helping your Big Ü to grow. It's helped to keep us safe and got some of our needs met. It's danced with our soul and helped us to find and make our place in the world.

The ego keeps us grounded, balanced and moving at a comfortable pace. Either before or after reading this book, the ego has accepted the notion of interconnected consciousness.

Hopefully the ego is also comfortable that it virtually disappears, and has no real place or purpose, in Oneness. If this sounds like a road to self-termination, there is no need to worry.

Our ego is like the child in the playground of the Material World. Children like to play with other children, so let your ego out to play. Children like to play with toys, too, so surround yourself with playthings.

This playful ego differs from the smaller ego that you possessed as a real child. It is not jealous of the toys of other children. Neither does it need to brag about its own toys.

Your Big Ego is not a big ego. It is a source-ress

or source-rer, where the source is the Oneness. The toys are trinkets in the Material World that you use to play with Duality and invoke and tap into Superconsciousness.

This ego is having fun showing Oneness what is possible in the Material World. Here the dreams can get dreamier. Ask for a superpower but be mindful of what you want to use it for.

For example, each of us has the ability to channel healing energy. If this is your thing, it should be used to heal and not necessarily to make a fortune.

How 3: Be here now

As we embrace Oneness, we realise the purpose of each why, how and energy in the previous parts of the book.

They were all mindfully designed and created to bring you to this place, right now. They have helped you take your golden thread apart and make it whole again. Nobody else has done this for you. You are solely responsible for bringing yourself to this place.

Once your golden thread is rewoven, the path ahead is made for you. While you might think you can take your foot of the gas, it brings a new responsibility. You are required to be constantly present and in the moment.

You have to be mindful of all thoughts, feelings and actions. In this place, mindfully not taking any action is equally as valid as taking an action. A Big Ü knows when the time is right. If your gut advises caution, or your heart isn't in it, your head will be foolhardy to overrule.

A Big Ü should not be swayed by either a small ü with a tempting proposition, or by someone you might perceive to be a Bigger Ü. All Big Ü's are intrinsically as big as each other. They are also just as big as a small ü too. It's just that a small ü hasn't yet woken up to exactly how big it is.

You are only who you are now, and where you are, because of what has gone before. Therefore, everything ahead of you is completely dependent on what you do, feel and think right now.

That's quite a big thought but also a nice and easy one. If a thought comes along that you are not happy with, ask it to go away because you're busy. If it's a small thought, ask for a bigger one to replace it. In Superconsciousness, there's an infinity of thoughts to choose from after all.

How 4: Being a Big Ü

As a child learns to swim, they might start out with the help of inflatable armbands. They will also be in the shallow end of a swimming pool so that they can put their feet down should they take in a mouthful of water.

In time, the armbands come off and the child can swim widths. At any time, their feet can touch the floor. There comes a time though when they swim their first length of the pool. For at least half of their journey, they have to really swim or they might sink. Their belief and satisfaction develops as they realise the deep end is not so scary after all.

When your Big Ü takes its first steps, it is wise to make them really small steps. Always make sure you can get back to the safety of where you came from. Each time you venture out, go a little further and deeper.

At the same time as you get out more physically in the Material World, take equal steps out into Duality and Superconsciousness.

In Duality, notice disparities and make fair what is unjust. Don't do this in protest but by taking action. Remember that quiet power is more powerful.

To dive deeper into Superconsciousness, if you have been meditating for 10 minutes a day, try

20 minutes. If you've been listening to guided meditations, try silent meditation.

Be mindful each day that you are an expression of Oneness having fun in the Material World. So each day, have more fun doing something bigger.

You will soon find that you then get called to step up more and more. The people who used to be around you get replaced by souls having a greater adventure. You will end up having so much fun that it is easy to forget that you've left some good friends back in the shallow end. Go back and hold their hand and show them how you are being a Big Ü.

Energy 1: Being of service

We are all incredibly lucky to be who we are. This luck that we are graced and blessed with is nicely infectious.

Our very being affects everything around us and whatever we choose to connect with. Just by being your Big Ü enables others to become their Big Ü.

Our Big Ü provides an environment for creativity, expansion and connectedness. We become a role model for others to follow. We become fully present with others when they recognise we are coming from our heart and soul. We see them as they are, accept who they are and, in our presence, they open up even further.

The old ego has no place in here as the Big Ego knows they have merely stepped up to what they were called to do. They have entered service but this service starts by serving their own needs.

Nobody can love, breathe or think for anybody else. A Big Ü looks after their own physical, emotional and spiritual requirements first and then, and only then, encourages others to do the same. If help is needed by others, it is given either freely or in exchange for other energies, such as money, goodwill or by skill swap and barter.

This way the bank accounts of everyone,

be they based on currency, bitcoins or karma points, increase together.

The collective bank of the Superconsciousness grows too. Even unconsciously, others you have never met can tap into what you've learned.

It is the duty and purpose of a Big Ü to share, to give, to help, to love and to enable others to grow. This way everyone can make the most of their lives. Giving in this way feeds us and feeds others. Every one benefits and every one grows and the Oneness smiles at what it has created in the Material World.

All the Big Ü has done is to show up as a being of service.

Energy 2: Leaving breadcrumbs

Over the last few hundred years, humankind has had the smarts to extend their longevity with education, nutrition, sanitisation and advances in the field of medicine.

Many people can now expect to have greatly extended working lives, which opens up opportunities for achieving far more at every level and at every stage of our lives. We can now transform our thinking so that we take full advantage of these opportunities to open our minds, our hearts and our souls further and deeper than our ancestors ever did.

We can now think of long-term solutions and opportunities, rather than short-term fixes. If we are going to be working several decades longer than our parents, we need to be even more certain that we are doing jobs that we love. Ideally they might move humankind forward towards a happier and more successful place.

Governments are beginning to wake up and tackle behaviours that affect the whole planet. Over the first half of this century, we will all start driving electric cars and our waste will be increasingly recycled and reused. This is happening already and will leave a great legacy for our children. They should be proud of what their parents did.

THE BIG Ü

When it comes to leaving a mark, we don't have to wait for legislation before taking action. The best time to plant a tree is today and the second best time is tomorrow.

Our legacy is not just what we leave behind on our last day on Earth. It starts from what we do while we are here. It is natural that a Big Ü will want to make a big impact and leave a big legacy behind.

To do this, all that is needed is to drop a breadcrumb a day to make a big long trail.

Energy 3: Becoming a conduit

Having found your Big Ü, you may wake up one morning and find yourself with a blank day ahead of you. You can awaken without any goals and without a to-do list to do.

As you step into your day, events unfold and you don't react, you respond. If people ask something of you and you cannot help them, politely say no but suggest where they might look for assistance. If you can help, then drop what you are doing and give them a hand.

If you are by yourself and a thought comes your way, ask who sent it and for what purpose, and act on the answer.

If you really find yourself at a loose end, with no direction, go out for a walk or a drive somewhere at random and see where you end up. You will end up, in your thoughts and feelings and in space and time, somewhere new.

If, however, you have a sense of direction and know what your Big Ü is tasked with doing, ignore all the above. If people make demands on your time and attention, tell them politely you are busy and ask whether you can speak to them later. Carry out your tasks with gusto, joy and aplomb and allow the energies of prescience and precognition to flow freely through you.

In time, and with practice, your Big Ü will be so

much in flow that your thought stream will fuse with the Superconsciousness. This of course is one of the aspects of Oneness, when you are no longer working in isolation but in a mode where you are fully connected.

When the above connects to the below through your Big Ü, you become a conduit with your heart as the pivot point.

This is truly the point where your Big Ü fully shows up in the world.

Energy 4: Always open

In some spiritual practices and circles, acolytes are taught how to open up their energy centres to receive and transmit when engaged in their practice. When they have done whatever they are taught or called to do, they are then told to close their energy centres down again. This kind of teaching comes from a position of fear and perhaps a little caution.

A Big Ü operates with an always-on and always-open approach. When you are taught to close down you pick up a so-called 'negative energy'. What is actually happening is the fear that you might pick it up is actually generating that unwanted energy. It self-serves to generate the opposite effect to that which is desired.

When you start your day, from a heart-based position of unconditional love, what happens is that love energy just comes your way continually and you beam it out again. As it happens, there is no such thing in the entire cosmos as 'negative energy', it is just positive energy not quite pointing in the optimal direction.

Someone at work who is disruptive is actually really intelligent and creative. It's just that their creativity is not being channelled as best as it might be.

Alchemy is the art of transmutation, turning

lead into gold being a metaphorical example. A Big Ü can always see the bright side and turn pessimism into optimism. Where it sees anger and frustration, it knows how to turn that around so that it creates a desire to do something about it. Any action will come from a place of quiet power.

A Big Ü can also see when people are being creative for creativity's sake and not actually delivering anything tangible as a result of their busyness. Here Oneness and Superconsciousness are temporarily disconnected from Duality and the Material World.

A Big Ü is an energy alchemist who is fully open to all possibilities.

KEY TAKEAWAYS

Everything was once one.
Everything still is one.
Each and every thought and deed matters.
Each of us is capable of being the change.

COMPANION MEDITATION: REACHING ONENESS

This meditation can be listened to lying down or sitting up or even with your eyes open and out walking in nature. It takes you on a guided journey from the centre of your being to the outer cosmos—and back again.

QUESTIONS TO PONDER

Why are you here?
What will be your legacy?
What makes you unique?
How do you know when your soul is guiding you?

THE BIG Ü

The Path Ahead

STEPPING UP TO being a Big Ü might at first sound and appear to be a little onerous. After all you might well have enough on your plate. It is our intention, and experience, however that it is an easier way to be.

It is less stressful and more effortless for the real you to come forward into the world. All the energy that was previously spent maintaining a pretence, and watching your back, fade away.

When you become an expression of Oneness in the Material World, life becomes a breeze. You will find that loving unconditionally is less stressful than management of any conditions set around giving and receiving love. You become comfortable with the notion of loving yourself first and how this puts you in a better position to give more love to and receive more love from others.

You will discover that regularly treating yourself to time out facilitates you being able to fully commit to times when your attention is needed. It is in these moments of quietness that your soul can guide you with whispers of insight and gentle instruction. This guidance that arrives in this way is invaluable, like gold dust.

Everything you need starts to show up at the perfect time and in the most sublime manner. As unrequited wants, desires and needs diminish, we become less stressed about what we thought might be missing from our lives. We realise not only that we have all we need but also that we have the ability to conjure up any lack.

The key is to always be mindful of the location of your awareness.

The Material World is a place for adventure and experience. Here our ego experiences highs and lows, fun and sadness and excitement and fear.

Duality is the plane of awareness and witness. We see disparity and unfairness here. At the same time we notice how only a subtle shift in perspective is required to bring about parity and to make imbalances fair. How full or empty is that glass after all?

The seed ideas that bring such enlightenment come from Superconsciousness. This plane connects us to our soul essence and our reason to be. When we start walking our true path, we show up in the world authentically and with grace. The weight of the world lifts when we can at last be truthful and honest, with both ourselves and others.

When we truly align with Oneness, we at last take conscious control over our destiny. More accurately we allow our destiny to play out under our observation. This is the nature of living in a Material World based on Duality. We are both conscious that we are making choices and allowing choices to be made. We are comfortable that some choices might at first seem like mistakes but that, in time, they open up new opportunities and lead us to new pastures.

When we allow Oneness to blossom and flower in the Material World, our soul at last steps forward. No longer are we able to play it small. Playing it big however does not mean that we play it loud. Neither does this process produce a large number of Big Ü clones. This path leads each of us to our own truth and to a position where we can discover and express our uniqueness.

While you are in transition to this new way of being, at all times be mindful of your internal and external language.

Be the heart and soul of the party. Only make decisions based on gut instinct. Put your heart into everything you do. Put your best foot forward and keep your head held high.

About Laurence

LAURENCE WAS FORCED to discover his Big Ü at a very early stage. He was afflicted by the different-ability of dyslexia at school in the 1960s and 70s. The condition was not understood or recognised so he felt he had to find a way of being recognised and accepted by his peers, both inside and outside of academia.

Laurence realised that, despite being a natural introvert, he had the knack of connecting to people by understanding what made them tick. This allowed him to discover how he could best help them. His 'different wiring' became his strength as he could see the world through a different lens.

In the 80s and 90s, Laurence developed his natural talents by gaining an understanding of human thinking, behaviour and influential leadership. His Big Ü worked alongside key players from the most forward-thinking companies where he gained the respect of business leaders and their teams. They were 'all ears' to his different approach.

With Amanda, he set up the Udell Group over 20 years ago to support business leaders, entrepreneurs, influencers, high performers and high net worth individuals all over the world.

He helped them overcome difficult challenges, maximise their performance and deliver results over and above expectation.

He has developed many growth and transformational tools which combine western business models with eastern spiritual techniques. With them, Laurence has been able to empower people and their organisations to produce profound results.

His premise, and real 'bigness', is that by 'waking up' to our soul we raise our consciousness and we can begin to understand our true meaning and purpose.

This in turn enables us to perform at our very best and live the life we love.

About Tom

TOM EVANS IS an author, meditation guide and expert at using mindfulness techniques for real world outcomes. Tom's Big Ü was shown to him. He was and is lucky in this regard. Like many in this boat though, it took him many years to realise what was going on.

In his early career, he was shown he had a flair for understanding, explaining and utilising high technology. At first this was in the broadcast TV industry and latterly with the Interweb.

In his mid-40s, the wheels came off a rather comfortable bus after his second business exit. A rather stressed version of Tom started to question the point of it all.

He was introduced to meditation and the world of metaphysics and the pennies began to drop. He wrote a short book by accident in a 747 at 39,000 feet above the Atlantic and a new world opened up when he landed. Within a year, he discovered a new career an author's mentor. This lead him become adept with some coaching and therapeutic tools.

Books then started to flow through him at a rate of more than one a year. Many were accompanied by meditations which Tom at first saw as accessories to his writing.

A few years back, his meditations were discovered, and made available worldwide, by the Insight Timer app. It took a million listens for Tom to realise they were actually quite good. It dawned on him that he had evolved into being a meditation teacher who happened to be a writer.

Throughout this transition, the engineer in Tom has been active. His real 'bigness' is in explaining the unexplainable and giving people access to the inaccessible. He likes to call it making the esoteric exoteric.

This is his essence.

Next Steps

WE HOPE YOU have learned that the discovery of your Big Ü is all about the journey. This is a journey where there is no particular end point but many joyous way points along the way to drop in upon.

Reading the book is one of these way points but equally important is listening to the companion meditations. If you haven't listened to them yet, here's a reminder of where to get hold of them:

http://thebigu.me/companion-meditations

From this book and these meditations, it is our hope and aim that you find a new sense of freedom from some the contradictions that living in a Material World underpinned by the Duality.

When you then open the door and readily tap into Superconsciousness and merge with Oneness, you become increasingly able to operate from a place of unconditionality. This allows you to truly step into your quiet power.

If you are interested in stepping everything up a gear or three, we have developed three programmes for those who are intrigued in exploring how big their Ü can actually get.

Firstly, our Biggest Ü programme is a set of personally mentored steps, taken over a number of months, that facilitate the embodiment of your soul. At the end of this process, you truly step into a new way of feeling, doing and being.

Secondly, people around you might want to know how and why you have stepped into such a magical way of being. For any coaches, consultants and leaders who are interested in helping others take these steps, our Biggest Ü programme is the precursor to our practitioner training.

Thirdly, and as we mentioned, when a number of Big Ü's start working together in the same business, their bigness scales exponentially. Our Team Ü programme is designed to guide groups of people to discover new ways of working and operating.

Get in touch if you want to know more, or just fancy a chat.

http://thebigu.me/contactus

Big Love from Laurence and Tom

Lightning Source UK Ltd.
Milton Keynes UK
UKHW02f0859160818
327336UK00012B/1254/P

9 781912 014446